Race and Curriculum:
Social Inequality and the Theories and Politics of Difference in Contemporary Research on Schooling

Race and Curriculum:
Social Inequality and the
Theories and Politics of
Difference in Contemporary
Research on Schooling

Cameron McCarthy

 The Falmer Press

(A member of the Taylor & Francis Group)

London • New York • Philadelphia

UK   The Falmer Press, Rankine Road, Basingstoke, Hampshire, RG24 0PR

USA   The Falmer Press, Taylor & Francis Inc., 1900 Frost Road, Suite 101, Bristol, PA 19007

First published 1990

British Library Cataloguing in Publication Data

McCarthy, Cameron.
 Race and curriculum: social inequality and the theories and politics of difference in contemporary research on schooling.
 1. United States. Education. Racial discrimination. I. Title.
 370.193420973
 ISBN 1-85000-682-2
 ISBN 1-85000-683-0 (pbk.)

Library of Congress Cataloging-in-Publication Data

McCarthy, Cameron.
 Race and curriculum: social inequality and the theories and politics of difference in contemporary research on schooling/by Cameron McCarthy.
   p.   cm.
 Includes bibliographical references and index.
 ISBN 1-85000-682-2   ISBN 1-85000-683-0 (pbk.).
 1. Minorities—Education—United States. 2. Education—Social aspects—United States. 3. Race awareness—United States 4. Curriculum change—United States. 5. Educational equalization—United States. I. Title.
 LC3731.M38   1990
 371.97′00973—dc20   90-43914
                                                        CIP

Jacket design by Caroline Archer

Typeset in 11/13pt Bembo by
Graphicraft Typesetters Ltd, Hong Kong

Printed in Great Britain by Burgess Science Press, Basingstoke on paper which has a specified pH value on final paper manufacture of not less than 7.5 and is therefore 'acid free'.

Contents

List of Figures

Acknowledgments

Though the act of writing is often portrayed as the most private and individual of endeavors (the 'author' locked away in a 'small combustible room'), my experience in writing *Race and Curriculum* was somewhat different. I should think that without the insights, encouragement and support of my editor Laura Stempel Mumford and my friends and colleagues, the book might not have been written at all. The members of my doctoral committee at the University of Wisconsin-Madison, Michael Apple, Elizabeth Ellsworth, Herbert Kliebard, Thomas Streeter and Roberta Astroff were particularly supportive and offered valuable criticism and guidance.

Many of the ideas that were eventually developed and fleshed out in *Race and Curriculum* were first tried and tested in the now famous Michael Apple Friday Group Meetings. Besides Michael, special thanks are due to the following members of the Friday Group: Sabiha Ansa, Marie Brennan, Hank Bromley, Pat Burdell, Alexandra Burton-James, Kathleen Casey, Seewa Cho, David Hursh, Hiro Inokuchi, Bruce King, Jim Ladwig, Maria Soledad Martinez, Betsy May, Susan Nofke, Bu Kwon Park, Nancy Riley and Joyce Shanks.

But at Madison there was that additional phenomenon — a band of maroon or renegade graduate student intellectuals, the closely-knit participants of the Moruzso Sessions, Ahmad Sultan, Marie Brennan, and Avanthia Milingou — whose watchwords, 'Instant deconstruction!' and 'Never keep your powder dry!' echoed around the world. The Moruzso Wednesday evening confabs, though always marked by unfettered, spirited and fiery contention, also evinced a rare spirit of camaraderie and solidarity that I will never forget. Having one session a week where I could 'cut loose' among friends worked like therapy and boosted my writing considerably.

I should also express my gratitude to my colleague and friend

Acknowledgments

Warren Crichlow at the University of Rochester who all this while has kept me literate, generously supplying me with the latest insights on race and culture published in such alternative journals as *Art Forum*, *Screen* and the *Village Voice*.

Special thanks are due to my graduate students and colleagues at Louisiana State University, Brenda Hatfield, Susan Edgerton, Tony Molina, Robert McDonald, John St. Julien, Noel Hammat, Angela Lyndon, Linda Stelly, Bill Pinar and Leslie Roman, who read drafts of my manuscript at various stages and offered many useful insights.

Finally, I am deeply indebted to Stuart Hall who, at a very early stage of my writing, was very direct in his encouragement: 'Now that you know what you know, it is time to get on with it Cameron!'

Preface

But, paradoxically, the category of 'race' alone cannot provide an adequate explanation of racism. . . . Race is a phenomenon which one only begins to understand when one sees it working within different institutions, processes and practices of whole societies, in their full complexity. (Hall, 1981, pp. 59–60)

Pascal: Tercerons, blacks, marabouts, mamelukes, griffons, quarterons, sacatras, mulattoes! They're all demanding rights; we'll never see the end of it! (Glissant, 1981, p. 29)

As we enter the decade of the 1990s in the United States, we are witnessing a radical intensification of neo-conservative offensives within the major social and cultural institutions of American society: the courts, the church, and alas, the schools. This intensification within the arenas of what some radical theorists call the 'superstructures' (Omi and Winant, 1986) is indicative of a considerable enlargement of areas of social conflict. Contestation among embattled social groups now extends well beyond the arenas that radical educators and curriculum theorists have traditionally been inclined to link with schooling, namely, the workplace and 'the' economy (Laclau and Mouffe, 1985). These areas of conflict have extended throughout the culture as a whole, and revolve around such issues as racial inequality, gender bias, nuclear weapons and environmental pollution, just to mention some of the main themes.

Over the last decade or so, there has also been an enlargement of the cast of publicly designated, politically relevant combatants — the 'new' social movements of racial minorities, immigrant groups, women, gays and lesbians, and that highly motivated and eager cast of religious and cultural neo-conservatives (the Moral Majority, the Eagle Forum, the Gablers and so on) who have targeted the school curriculum and the education system as crucial sites for struggle over issues of 'reverse discrimination' and school prayer. In some ways, the decade of the 1980s can be described as the neo-conservative decade — a period in which neo-conservative forces, led by a deeply committed Republican administration and an ideologically stacked Supreme Court, have, with considerable success, sought to redraw the map of social liberties and civil rights in the United States with respect to the national flag, abortion, racial quotas in the labor market, race-conscious recruitment in the university system, and so on.

These events in social and political life have been associated with particularly painful developments in American schools and college campuses: minority levels of achievement and rates of graduation are declining at the same time that these educational institutions have become battlegrounds for racial strife and the vilification and harassment of minority youth. As problems associated with racial antagonism and minority underachievement intensify in schools, contemporary educators and curriculum theorists seem somewhat overtaken by events.

In *Race and Curriculum*, I try to put into a broader theoretical and political perspective the thorny issues of racial inequality and minority underachievement now facing educators in schools and universities across the country. After presenting a critical overview of mainstream and radical accounts and programmatic 'solutions' to racial inequality in education, I will offer an alternative approach, which I will call a *nonsynchronous theory* of race relations in schooling. In advancing such a theory, I will maintain that the persistence of racial inequality in education cannot be properly accounted for by reference to a single-causal logic. Neither mainstream educators' prioritization of cultural values and prejudice, as in the multicultural models of Tiedt and Tiedt (1986) and others, nor radical theorists' insistence on the determinant role of labor market segmentation (Edari, 1984) in the shaping of social differences, provide us with a sufficient explanation of current developments in race relations in the United States.

Instead, I direct attention to the complex nature of race relations in the institutional life of social organizations such as schools. Rather than treating minority groups as homogeneous entities, I point to the contradictory interests, needs and desires that inform minority social, educational and political behavior and define minority encounters with majority whites in educational settings. These discontinuities in the needs and interests of minority and majority groups are, for example, expressed in the long history of tension that has existed between the black and white working class in this country. Also of crucial importance within this framework is the issue of 'the contradictory location' (Wright, 1978) of the 'new' black middle class within the racial problematic and the role of neoconservative black and white intellectuals in redefining the terrain of contemporary discourse on racial inequality toward the ideal of a 'color blind' society. Just as important for a theory of nonsynchrony is the fact that minority women and girls have radically different experiences of racial inequality from those of their male counterparts (Grant, 1984).

My principal theoretical concern in what follows is therefore to stress the importance of social context and nuance in understanding the dynamics of race relations. I also emphasize the need to pay attention to the differential patterns of historical and contemporary incorporation of minority and majority groups into the social and cultural relations that exist in the school setting. Such a complex understanding of racial differences in education can help us to better formulate policies and strategies of reform that will address the difficult problems associated with the unequal race relations that now exist in American schools.

Cameron McCarthy
1990

Chapter 1

Introduction: Race and Curriculum

It is not altogether surprising to find a certain uneven development within the various branches of social science disciplines
. . . It could be argued that race analysis is surprisingly back-
ward in this respect, far more so, for instance, than recent
debates within the feminist movement. (Ben-Tovim, Gabriel,
Law and Stredder, 1981, p. 155)

Marxist and other progressive writers on Africa generally
approach the issue of 'tribalism' as one would approach a
minefield. (Saul, 1979, p. 131)

The problems of racial antagonism and racial inequality continue to
plague societies in the developed modernized world, such as England,
Australia and the United States. It is precisely these societies that
classical sociologists had assured us would witness a rapid and drastic
decline in racial and ethnic particularism (Omi and Winant, 1986; Rex,
1983). Contemporary evidence in the evolving decade of the 1990s in
the United States, however, tells a different story. And as one social
and economic crisis after another threatens to engulf minority communities, it has become clear that racial inequality is a far more
permanent and stable phenomenon in post-industrial societies than
sociologists such as Marx or Weber had imagined.
   Yet despite comprehensive evidence of glaring disparities in
education in the United States, theorists have been slow in developing
rigorous, durable, or compelling explanations of the reproduction and
persistence of racial/ethnic inequality[1] in schooling. In sharp contrast,
American curriculum theorists and sociologists of education have been
far more forthcoming in their examination of the ways in which the
variables of class and, more recently, gender have informed the

organization and selection of school knowledge and the production and reproduction of subcultures among school youth (Anyon, 1983; Apple and Beyer, 1988; Apple and Weis, 1983; Bowles and Gintis, 1976; Everhart, 1983). To put the matter forthrightly, and as black sociologists such as Mullard (1985) have pointed out, both mainstream and radical educational researchers have tended to undertheorize and marginalize phenomena associated with racial inequality (Sarup, 1986). Of course, this is not to deny the fact that there is a growing 'interest' in race in the curriculum and educational literature (Troyna and Williams, 1986). But as we shall see, current mainstream and radical curriculum and educational theories do not adequately address or account for the persistence of racial inequality in schooling.

In *Race and Curriculum*, I directly address the issue of the theoretical status of the race category in curriculum and educational research. I should say before I move on that in appraising the curriculum and educational literature, I will in fact be discussing two separate traditions of research on unequal relations in schooling: *curriculum theory* and *sociology of education*. While I recognize that there is often considerable tension and discontinuity between these traditions, I believe the commonalities in their analyses of racial inequality in education are worth stressing. I will therefore be using the terms 'curriculum theory' and 'sociology of education' interchangeably and non-paradigmatically throughout. I will specifically direct attention to the following questions: How have mainstream and radical American educators, curriculum theorists and sociologists of education sought to explain racial inequality in schooling? What indeed is the relationship of race to the modern school curriculum and how should this relationship be theorized in order to give us greater explanatory purchase on the nature and effects of racial inequality? More importantly, what type of principles should guide current and future approaches to the reform of race relations in education?

Events in the past decade in education and society in the United States and elsewhere have made the study of questions concerning the persistence of racial inequality in schooling particularly urgent. Three factors stand out. First and most ominous is the looming specter of racial conflagration and recrimination in high schools and on college campuses across the country. Attacks on minority students on northern college campuses such as Wisconsin-Madison, California-Berkeley, Massachusetts-Amherst and Michigan have caused considerable alarm, since these universities had built reputations in the 1960s as havens for African-American youth wishing to escape the more notorious racism of southern universities (Lord, 1987; Steele,

1989; Tifft, 1989; Viadero, 1989).[2] A second major issue of concern is the persistent evidence of intolerable levels of minority failure and alienation from schooling — this despite mainstream programs and policies ostensibly aimed at ameliorating racial differences in education (Cortes, 1986; Ogbu and Matute-Bianchi, 1986). Third, these intolerable levels of minority underachievement are occurring precisely at a time when school populations in the United States are becoming more ethnically diverse. In the state of California, for example, the majority of children now attending elementary schools are racial minorities. Forty-six per cent of the students in Texas are black and Hispanic. In the twenty-five largest city school systems 'the majority of the students are minorities' (*Education Week*, 14 May 1986, p. 16). This demographic trend in schools is also reflected in statistics on the general population. Current projections suggest that by 'the turn of the century, one out of every three Americans will be non-white' (*Education Week*, 14 May 1986, p. 15).

But these issues go much further than numbers and percentages. These developments in schools and in the general population are themselves imbricated in historical processes of socioeconomic and demographic change which have accelerated during the postwar period and whose consequences have become particularly pronounced in recent years. Some of the most evident of these dynamics include the following: a general shift in the economy from goods-producing to service-intensive industries; an increasing bifurcation of the labor market into low-wage/high-wage sectors, or what is more generally known in the social science literature as labor market segmentation; technological innovation, for example, automation and robotics; the relocation out and/or de-industrialization of the manufacturing sectors of central cities; and a reconstitution of the social composition of the work force, which now consists mainly of women and minorities (Crichlow, 1985, 1990; Swinton, 1988). Not only have these rapid developments altered the nature of what is sometimes crudely designated as 'the' economy, but they have helped to define the nature of race relations and society in the 1980s in the United States, and have set the tone for the 1990s as well.

As schools have begun to mediate these dramatic changes taking place in the socioeconomic fabric of the society, evidence of inequality has become quite alarming. Recent statistics on racial inequality deserve a moment of contemplation. Mounting evidence supplied in government commission reports, academic journals and census data documents gross disparities in the relative educational and socioeconomic fortunes of racial minorities vis-a-vis whites in the United States.

Indeed, current statistics indicate stagnation and in some cases reversals of minority fortunes since the gains of the civil rights movement in the 1960s and the early 1970s (Jacob, 1988). For example, in the decade-and-a-half since 1975, overall unemployment has averaged 15.2 per cent for black Americans. The rate of unemployment for whites for the same period is 6.0 per cent. Indeed, the ratio of black-to-white unemployment throughout the 1980s 'averaged well over the traditional two-to-one historical ratio' (Swinton, 1988, p. 147). In 1986, the median income for black families was 57.1 per cent of that of white families — some three percentage points less than it was in 1970! The Alliance Against Women's Oppression (1983) contends in one of their discussion papers that black mothers are four times as likely to die at childbirth as white mothers. Black and Native American infant mortality rates are currently higher than those of Third World countries such as Costa Rica and Trinidad and Tobago (Alliance Against Women's Oppression, 1983, pp. 1–8).

This pattern of severe black disadvantage is also reflected in the statistical information now available on racial inequality in schooling in the United States. Hann, Danzberger and Leftkowitz (1987), the authors of *Dropouts in America*, a recent report prepared for the Institute for Educational Leadership, contend that in 1986 40 per cent of Hispanic and 28 per cent of black students had dropped out of high school, compared with 13 per cent of white high school youth. Today, there are fewer black high school graduates entering colleges than there were in 1976. In the decade-and-a-half since 1976, the proportion of black high school graduates who go on to college has declined from 33.5 per cent to 26 per cent. And of those black students who make it to college, only 42 per cent continue on to graduation (Sudarkasa, 1988).

These statistics are indeed disturbing. They trenchantly underscore the intractability of racial inequality in school and society in the United States. But racial inequality of this sort is not peculiar to America. In other urban industrialized societies, such as England, Japan, Canada and Australia, research has shown that minority youth also fare poorly in school and in the labor market (Ogbu and Matute-Bianchi, 1986).

Over the years, mainstream and radical curriculum theorists and sociologists of education have provided contrasting explanations for the persistence of racial inequality in schooling. On the one hand, mainstream educators have tended to reduce the complexities associated with racial inequality to one overwhelming concern: *the issue of the educability of minorities*. In these accounts the central task has been to explain perceived differences between black and white students as reflected in differential achievement scores on standardized tests, high school drop-out rates, and so on. Explanations of black 'underachievement' are consequently situated within pathological constructions of minority cognitive capacities (Dunn, 1987; Jensen, 1981), child-rearing practices (Bell, 1975), family structures (Moynihan, 1965), and linguistic styles (Hess and Shipman, 1975; Orr, 1987). (For an extended discussion of these pathological approaches, see Henriques, 1984.) Mainstream theorists have in this sense tended to 'blame the victim'. Curriculum practices and interventions predicated on these approaches attempt to influence positive changes in minority school performance through the manipulation of specific school variables, such as teacher behavior, methods of testing, placement, counseling and so forth (Atkinson, Morten and Sue, 1979; Cortes, 1986; Ogbu and Matute-Bianchi, 1986).

In contrast to mainstream emphasis on values and behavior, neo-Marxist sociologists such as Bowles and Gintis (1976), Edari (1984), Jackubowicz (1985) and Nkomo (1984) locate the roots of racial inequality within the structural properties of capitalism and its elaboration as a world system. Racial inequality in these accounts is something of a by-product of the major class contradiction between labor and capital. These radical school critics subsume the problem of racial inequality under the general rubric of working-class oppression. They contend that there is a structural relationship between a racially differentiated school curriculum and a discontinuous labor market. A number of neo-Marxist sociologists of education have therefore sought to explain minority failure by reference to the role the education system plays in producing and supplying the passive, trainable recruits required in the secondary labor market. In this story, schools follow the pattern of the economy. Thus, these school critics offer no programmatic solution to the problem of racial domination: the latter will disappear with the abolition of capitalism.

It must of course be pointed out, as I have indicated elsewhere (McCarthy and Apple, 1988), that there is considerable nuance and variation within both mainstream and radical accounts of race and schooling. Generally, though, mainstream and radical conceptualizations of the relationship between race and schooling diverge. Mainstream educators emphasize the causal role of values and individual agency, while neo-Marxist sociologists point to the structural relationship between schools and the economy and its 'needs' for various types of skilled and semi-skilled labor. I will offer an alternative formulation that attempts to avoid privileging either 'cultural values' or 'economic structures' as 'the' exclusive or unitary source of racial inequality in schooling.

Parallelism and Nonsynchrony: Beyond Essentialist Accounts of Race Relations in Schooling

In significant ways, then, both mainstream and radical conceptualizations of racial inequality are 'essentialist' in that they effectively eliminate the 'noise' of multidimensionality, historical variability and subjectivity from their explanations of educational differences (Omi and Winant, 1986; Troyna and Williams, 1986; West, 1988). Current approaches to racial inequality tend to rely too heavily on linear, single-causal models or explanations that retreat from the exploration of the political, cultural and economic contexts in which racial groups encounter each other in school and in social life. Cortes (1986) points to these limitations in his examination of current approaches to racial inequality in education:

> Some analyses [of racial differences in education] have relied too heavily on single-cause explanations. Group educational differentials have been attributed, at various times, to language difference, to cultural conflict, to discriminatory instruments (such as IQ tests), or to the cultural insensitivity of educators. Yet as surely as one of these has been posited as 'the', or at least 'the principal', cause of group achievement differentials, then other situations are discovered in which these factors exist, and yet group achievement differentials do not occur ... There has been a tendency to decontextualize explanations. That is, explanations about the relationship between sociocultural factors and educational achievement often posit causation without consideration of the context in which these factors operate. (p. 16)

As Cortes points out, without an examination of institutional and social context it is difficult to understand how racial inequality operates in education. Current mainstream and radical conceptual frameworks do not effectively capture the heterogeneous and variable nature of race relations in either the school setting or society. Theoretical and practical insights that could be gained from a more relational and synthetic method of analyzing racial domination in education — one that attempts to show in detail the links between social structures (whether they be economic, political or ideological) and what real people such as teachers and students do — have been forfeited. It is exactly such a relational method that I will use to analyze current formulations on race and education. This approach will also provide the basic method for reformulating the relationship of race to schooling in a manner that at one and the same time affirms the autonomous effectivity of racial antagonism and also theorizes its vital connections to gender and to class oppression. Simply put, I will try to show that relations of class and gender are integral to the shaping of the racial character of contemporary schooling. As we will see, the intersection of these variables in the school environment complicates institutional dynamics and minority/majority relations considerably, particularly with respect to the incorporation and implementation of race relations reform.

I therefore approach the race/education couplet from the analytical perspective of the critical studies tradition at the radical neo-Marxist end of the sociology of schooling and the curriculum (Apple, 1986; Apple and Weis, 1983; Troyna and Williams, 1986; West, 1988). This critical approach emphasizes that there is a dynamic relationship between (a) the structural and institutional arrangements of school knowledge and the instrumental rules which constrain the educator and the educated alike, and (b) the self-affirming agency and capacities of social actors (teachers and students) to resist and transform the structural arrangements and relations that exist within educational settings and in the wider social milieu. Teachers and students do not simply capitulate to the unyielding demands of the economy or the constraints of instrumental rules formulated by the state, boards of education, and other centers of authority. I will argue, in part, that for better or worse, minority and majority school actors systematically reinvent and redirect structural and institutional requirements in their racial relationships with each other.

A new analysis of racial antagonism benefits from this critical tradition in the sociology of knowledge and schooling in the sense that the tradition directs us to the fact that racial domination is fundamentally secured in the cultural sphere. 'Culture' here is to be theorized and understood in the sense that Raymond Williams (1961, 1976) uses the concept; that is, the sensuous physical as well as symbolic process of production and reproduction of daily life across a variety of sites — the school, the home and the workplace. But it is the institution of schooling, as Althusser (1971) reminds us, that is principally organized around the production of knowledge and the production of meanings. It is schooling, via its instrumental (rules and bureaucratic organization) and expressive (rituals, etc.) orders, that generates and regenerates representations of the social world. In this context, a normative value system is elaborated in which students and teachers can affirm and locate themselves in relation to each other and to social actors outside the school. Schooling is thus fundamentally a site for the production and reproduction of social identities. It is in this sense, too, that 'difference' — defined here as the formal and informal operation of an assemblage of processes of separation, inclusion, exclusion and grouping — is inscribed in the *modus operandi* of school life.

Racial logics work through the structural and ideological organization of education, in textbooks, resource allocation and so forth. Schooling, for example, rationalizes minority failure via standardized achievement tests which privilege white middle-class values (Carby, 1982). These sorting and selecting processes are partly designed for, and certainly have the effect of, tracking students to differential careers in the outside world. Part of my contention is that schooling hooks up to the macrostructure and the economy through an autonomous discourse and language of 'achievement' and 'failure'. The expression of this autonomy has systematic racial effects in that the very identity and efficacy of individual schools are implicated in the effectiveness and normative force of these formal and informal rules of selection, grouping, rewards, sanctions and so on. It is precisely in this sense, then, that in the language of Rex (1983), schooling is a 'racializing context' or 'racial situation' (pp. 27–30). I will argue, for example, that the processes of selection that inform the daily pedagogical and curricular practices of schooling systematically disorganize minority identities by privileging white middle-class values. Minority alienation from the academic 'core' curriculum of schools, among other things, deprives minority students of the 'cultural capital' (Bordieu and Passeron, 1977) needed for access to middle-class jobs. But as we shall see, particularly when I discuss the multicultural education literature in Chapter 3, there are extra-school racial logics that operate in the labor market itself, such that artificially created racial ceilings constrain the job chances of minority youth (Ogbu, 1978; Ogbu and Matute-Bianchi, 1986).

A 'racial' curriculum as it is forged in schooling is therefore to be understood in terms of 'commodified' as well as 'lived' cultural practices (Apple, 1979). Such a 'reading' of the school curriculum will show that not merely economic, but cultural and political practices fundamentally shape the character of school life. But the matter goes further: schools are also thoroughly stratified by dynamics of class and gender as well as by race. One of the most effective presentations of this theoretical framework has been offered by Apple and Weis (1983) in terms of what they call 'the parallelist position'. In this parallelist approach, the authors argue that it is more helpful to conceptualize the social formation in terms of interlocking spheres of economy, politics and culture. Apple and Weis claim further that dynamic relations of race, class and gender interact with each other in complex ways, but that each is necessary for the mutual reproduction of the others. These arguments will be discussed in much greater detail in Chapter 5. But let me say here that perhaps the most significant contribution the parallelist approach has offered is that it has introduced into sociology of curriculum accounts a new way of understanding causation with respect to racial antagonism. Proponents of parallelism suggest that causal processes related to racial antagonism should no longer be located in a single theoretical space, namely, the structural properties of 'the' economy. Causal influences on racial antagonism are conceptualized as coming from a 'plurality' of processes operating simultaneously within the economic, cultural and political spheres of society. The parallelist approach therefore problematizes the elements of positivistic causal linearity which residually percolated within radical accounts of race and curriculum. In this sense, too, proponents of the parallelist position also avoid the tendency toward single-cause explanations of racial inequality so dominant among adherents of mainstream neo-correlational paradigms of educational research. Instead, these theorists point us toward the plurality of liabilities which handicap minority youth as raced, classed and gendered social subjects. This alternative model of multiple causation or 'overdetermination' is basically 'correct' and centrally informs my reformulation of the race/education couplet in Chapter 5.

But the parallelist approach to the analysis of social difference, while rejecting much of the reductionism and essentialism of earlier neo-Marxist structuralism, offers an 'additive' model of the intersection of race, class and gender which does not address issues of contradiction[3] and tension in schooling in any systematic way. Neither does it address the 'mix' of contingencies, interests, desires, needs, differential assets and capacities that exist in local settings such as schools. Thus, it does not offer us a clear enough insight into the specificity or directionality of effects of the intersection of race, class and gender in education.

In contrast to the parallelist theorists' emphasis on reciprocity and mutuality of effects, I will argue, as does Hicks (1981), that the intersection of race, class and gender in the institutional setting of the school is systematically contradictory or nonsynchronous and can lead to the augmentation or diminution of the effectivity of race, or for that matter, any other of these variables operating in the school environment. The concept of nonsynchrony summarizes the vast differences in interests, needs, desires and identity that separate different minority groups from each other and from majority whites in educational settings. I believe that it is necessary to offer theoretical arguments at a more conjunctural or middle level if we are to get a better handle on the way these dynamics operate in schools. Such an emphasis on nonsynchrony in the institutional context would help us to specify these dynamics of race and gender in a manner that would allow for an understanding of the multivocal, multi-accented nature of human subjectivity and the genuinely polysemic nature of minority/majority relations in education and society (Fiske, 1987).

There are already good examples of theoretical and practical work that have begun to explore the nonsynchronous interaction of race and other dynamics in the school setting. For instance, Mary Fuller (1980) points to such social contradictions and tensions in her study of the subculture of West Indian girls at a working-class high school in England. These students are shown to exist in a nonsynchronous relationship to their West Indian male counterparts and white working-class girls. While West Indian male youth rejected the school curriculum, the West Indian girls in Fuller's study were among the school's high achievers. However, their apparent compliance with school values of academic success paradoxically constituted the ideological basis for their assertion of 'independence' from West Indian boys, as well as their rejection of the racial label of 'underachievement' that the British school system applies to West Indian youth as a whole. It is studies like Fuller's, which sensitively treat the contradictions and tensions within the everyday practices of real raced, classed and gendered social actors such as teachers and students, that can help us make advances over the a-theoretical, single-group studies that now dominate the mainstream research on race and schooling. The key concepts of 'nonsynchrony' and 'contradiction' need to be fully integrated into radical approaches to race and curriculum.

At the same time, though, one needs to be careful not to fall back into a totally 'structural' reading of these issues. That is, we need to emphasize the symbolic, signifying, languaging dimensions of social interaction and their integral relationship to both systems of control and strategies for curricular reform.

An emphasis on symbols, signs and representation enables us to think through dynamics other than class (understood as an economic category) by directing our attention toward the processes of cultural selection, labeling and tracking that contribute directly to the formation and maintenance of differential racial and sexual identities in schooling and society. This has been particularly important for advancing our theoretical understanding of the ways in which racial and sexual antagonism operate within the cultural sphere and the ways in which racial and sexual differences are naturalized in everyday social practices. Indeed, it is important to remember that for a long time black and feminist writers have argued (much against the tide of dominant research) that racial antagonism and sexual oppression are mediated through ideology, culture, politics and social theories themselves. While some neo-Marxist theorists have maintained that it is economic exploitation and capitalist need for surplus value that explains the oppression of the socially disadvantaged and minority failure in schools, black and feminist writers have drawn attention to the devaluation of self-image, culture and identity. For writers such as Baldwin (1986), Ellison (1982), Jordan (1980) and Shange (1983), American schools are the principal sites for the production of myths, half-truths, silences and obfuscation about racially subordinated groups. It is with the full acknowledgment of the persuasiveness of these claims that race relations theorists such as West (1988) have argued that it is precisely in these 'non-economic' sites of self-production and identity formation, such as the school and the church, that African Americans and other minorities have sought to struggle against white oppression.

Only by taking these issues seriously within radical research frameworks can we overcome the past and present tendencies in mainstream and neo-Marxist scholarship which cultural critics such as Edward Said (1986, 1989) argue obliterate the specific histories and struggles of racially subordinated groups. This, of course, must be done with a full realization that culture and identity are produced in a material context. In the chapters that follow, I will argue that schooling is such a material context — a material context that is fundamentally racial in character. The fact that the principles of selection, inclusion and exclusion that inform the organization of school life have hitherto been understood through class and SES paradigms says more about the biographies of mainstream and neo-Marxist school theorists than about the necessary character of schooling. Any critical theoretical work on racial inequality in schooling must therefore involve some sober reflection on the racial character of the production of curriculum research itself.

But the issue of rethinking the racial order in American curriculum and school organization also leads us to the consideration of questions concerning pedagogical and political practice within education. Unless we focus on the issue of what can be done about racial inequality, given our critically informed analysis, we shall be left on the sidelines watching as the conservative restoration reconstructs education around its own principles of race, gender and class domination. As I will argue later in *Race and Curriculum*, critical theory must also be accompanied by a critical practice that links current concerns of teachers and students to larger issues of social inequality and social difference. Theories of how race, class and gender interact, and of how economic, political and cultural power act in education do need to become increasingly subtle, with a recognition of the important and variable roles that history, context and interests play in the articulation of relationships between minorities and dominant whites in the US. But we also need to remember what all of this theoretical labor is about — the political, economic and cultural lives of real people. Oppressed women and men and racially marginalized minority children are subject to relations of differential power. These relations are not abstract, but are experienced in ways that now help or hurt identifiable groups of people in all too visible ways. For this we do need conceptual and practical advances. By taking race and gender more seriously at all levels, we may make considerable movement beyond the limitations posed by existing theories and practices. Only in this way will we be able to go beyond the biological explanations of the conservatives, the individualistic and naively possibilitarian hopes of the liberals, and the almost cynical economistic positions of the orthodox Marxists.

Plan of the Book

In the preceding pages, I have attempted to situate current mainstream and radical debates on racial inequality within the context of present-day statistics on minority/majority fortunes in education and society in the United States of the emerging 1990s. I have also attempted to lay out the basic principles of an alternative approach to the race/education couplet — what I have called the non-synchronous position. This framework eschews single-cause explanations of racial differences in schooling. Instead, borrowing from some of the arguments presented by proponents of parallelist theory, I have sought to direct attention to the integral relationships that exists between the operation of racial antagonism and the variables of sexual and class oppression in the school environment. I have argued that the intersection of race, class and gender in cultural and ideological institutions such as schools is problematic, contingent and systematically contradictory or non-synchronous. This emphasis on contradiction, tension and multiple causation guides my appraisal of the current educational literature as well as my reformulation of the race/education couplet in the chapters that follow.

Chapter 2 focuses on the strengths, limitations and programmatic implications of current mainstream curriculum and educational research on the relationship of racial inequality to schooling. In particular, I explore the contradictions and tensions between biological and cultural explanations of differential school performance in the mainstream literature.

In Chapter 3, special attention is paid to the limits and possibilities of the value-oriented thesis of multiculturalism that mainstream liberal educators have championed within the last fifteen years or so as a panacea for racial antagonism in schooling.

Like the mainstream research on race, the radical literature is not monolithic in its discussion of social difference in education. In Chapter 4, I evaluate three different approaches to racial inequality in schooling within the radical neo-Marxist curriculum literature: 'structural economic', 'cultural reproduction' and 'critical curriculum theory'.

In Chapter 5, I offer an interim theory of racial domination that attempts to dissolve the unwarranted separation of considerations of 'values' from considerations of structural constraints on human action in current accounts of the race/education couplet. In this chapter, I develop arguments for the nonsynchronous position in greater detail. I also report and discuss ethnographic examples of nonsynchrony in race relations in schooling from the work of L. Grant (1984, 1985), Nkomo (1984) and Spring (1985).

Chapter 6, the final chapter, deals with my formulation of some broad democratic principles which I will argue can help to guide current policy approaches to race relations reform in schooling. Unfortunately, left educators have not directed enough attention to the crucial issue of educational policy. This has been particularly the case with respect to the subject of race relations. In Chapter 6, I try to lay the basis for a critical practice in the area of race-relations reform that directly draws on the conceptual advances on the state and education that are now being articulated by some radical cultural theorists (Cashmore and Troyna, 1990; Hall, 1988; Omi and Winant, 1986; Troyna and Williams, 1986).

Notes

1   As Omi and Winant (1986) have pointed out, there is a tendency within
    modern social theories of race relations to collapse the race category into
    the broader category of ethnicity. Race is thus understood as one of a
    number of determinants of ethnic group identity. 'Ethnicity' is defined by
    reference to concepts such as 'common culture', 'ancestry', 'language' and
    'interests'. This definition of ethnicity is primarily based on the experi-
    ences, patterns of association and mobilization historically relevant to
    white European immigrants to the United States. On the other hand, the
    concept of 'race' invokes physical differences as markers for designating
    'the great divisions of mankind', according to the *Oxford American Dic-
    tionary* (1980). I deliberately seek here to problematize these commonsense
    categories of the race/ethnic distinction. Race is therefore to be seen as an
    'unstable and "decentered" complex of social meanings constantly being
    transformed by political struggle' (Omi and Winant, 1986, p. 68). The
    conceptual significance of Omi and Winant's definition of race is that it
    recognizes the historical variability of the race category as an unstable
    ideological assemblage. By emphasizing the historicity of the concept,
    these writers avoid the trap of essentialism.
2   Twenty-five years after the landmark Civil Rights Act of 1964, schools
    and universities are experiencing what many educators now characterize
    as 'a disturbing resurgence of prejudice' (See Viadero, 1989, p. 6).
    According to the National Institute Against Prejudice and Violence, inci-
    dents of 'intergroup conflict' occurred at more than 160 colleges during
    the period 1986–1989. These incidents often involved conflicts between
    white students and blacks. Particularly notorious was the October 1986
    beating of a black student at the University of Massachusetts at Amherst
    after an argument about a World Series game turned into a racial attack
    with a crowd of some 3000 whites chasing twenty blacks. Other incidents
    of gross racial or ethnic insensitivity abound. At Yale University a swasti-
    ka and the words 'white power' were painted on the school's African
    American Cultural Center. And early in 1989, the University of
    Wisconsin-Madison chapter of the Zeta Tau Fraternity held a mock slave
    auction in which pledges painted their faces black and wore Afro wigs
    (Lord, 1987; Steel, 1989; Tifft, 1989).
3   I use the term 'contradiction' here and throughout in two senses. First,
    the use of contradiction is associated with a deconstructivist project that
    informs my study of race and education. I therefore draw attention to
    moments of rupture, discontinuity and structural silence in existing
    school practices and the social relations that define minority/majority
    encounters in education. For example, those moments of discontinuity
    and contradiction are articulated in the gap between the ostensible objec-
    tive of efficiency in school policies such as tracking and their unintended
    effects in terms of the marginalization of a large number of minority
    youth from an academic curriculum. Though educational administrators
    and teachers readily point to the 'fairness' of existing normative rules and
    criteria for assigning students to high/low academic tracks in school, the
    application of such normative rules (grades, standardized tests, etc.) pro-

cedurally constrain black access to genuine equality of opportunity in education. At the same time these rules benefit white middle-class youth, who have a clear advantage with respect to instructional opportunities, teacher time and material resources such as computers (Gamoran and Berends, 1986). In all-black schools, similar structural advantages can accrue to black middle-class students vis-a-vis their working-class counterparts, as Rist (1970) discovered. These 'built-in' discontinuities and contradictions exist as structural principles in everyday pedagogical and curriculum practices and profoundly influence minority encounters with whites in education. There is also a second, more positive application of the term contradiction. In this more Hegelian usage of the concept, I wish to suggest that it is precisely these discontinuities in minority/majority experiences in schooling that can provoke or motivate qualitative change and forward motion in social relations between blacks and whites. In this sense, I maintain that a genuine exploration of these contradictions in minority/majority education can help to lay the basis for meaningful race relations reform.

Mainstream Accounts of Racial Inequality in Schooling

In Chapter 1, I drew attention to the rather strong tendencies on the part of mainstream researchers to reduce the complex issues associated with racial inequality in schooling to the matter of the educability of minorities. I described this research orientation as 'essentialist' in the sense that in these mainstream accounts causal determination of racial inequality is ultimately assigned to biological and cultural deficits attributed to minority youth (Henriques, 1984; McCarthy and Apple, 1988; Troyna and Williams, 1986). One clear theoretical and pro-grammatic consequence of this research emphasis on biology and culture as explanatory concepts has been the tendency to insulate mainstream educational debates and policies on racial inequality in schooling from a discussion of the structural, economic and political dynamics that constrain and help shape the life chances of minority youth beyond the school. Instead, mainstream educators have tended to generate microlevel, process-product studies of educational differ-ences which focus on the impact of discrete variables such as teacher behavior, peer group interaction and instructional styles on minority educational achievement (Ogbu, 1978; Ogbu and Matute-Bianchi, 1986).

In this chapter, I will examine the strengths, limitations and im-plications of mainstream accounts of the race/education couplet. As we shall see, there are significant differences and discontinuities within current mainstream approaches to race and education. Mainstream literature, for instance, can be divided into conservative and liberal 'branches' (McCarthy and Apple, 1988). Broadly speaking, this divi-sion within mainstream frameworks expresses itself in terms of a tension between biological and cultural explanations of differential school performance. Although there is considerable variation within conservative approaches to schooling, as we will see when we discuss neo-conservative theories, conservative educators generally locate minority school failure in the innate psychological and biological capacities and characteristics of minority youth. Liberal educators and curriculum theorists have tended to eschew biological explanations of educational differences and point instead to differential cultural resources in the home, and so on, as explanatory variables in their accounts of minority failure (McLaren and Dantley, in press).

I would like to draw out these distinctions in more detail in what follows. But first, let me issue a caveat. In part, my classification of current educational research into categories of 'mainstream' and 'radical' or 'conservative' and 'liberal' does at times arbitrarily gloss over some of the important commonalities that exist among these bodies of theory. It is useful at times to call to mind some of these commonalities when we consider the curriculum and educational literature on racial inequality.

Modern American curriculum and educational theory (both radical and mainstream) share with classical social science theories certain genealogical origins with respect to a certain AngloEurocentrism. This was most powerfully expressed in a moral panic over the growing participation, in the late nineteenth century, of new social movements of immigrants and lower-class women and men in the institutional and political life of an emergent capitalist America (Hurn, 1979; Kliebard, 1986). Indeed, the evolution of modern social theory, as Foucault (1972, 1977) has told us, is implicated in discourses and practices of social regulation.[1] At the turn of the century, social and educational theorists such as Hall (1904), Mann (1957) and Ross (1901) waxed eloquent about the subversive potential of these new social developments in American society (Selden, 1985, 1988). Though I will expand on this theme of social regulation and control within mainstream educational research, I would now like to explore the nuances and contradictions in the mainstream literature in some detail.

As Wexler (1976) has pointed out, mainsteam educational research is not a unitary text. It embodies, along with its conservative tradition, a 'progressive possibilitarian' (Wexler, 1976) moment which has emphasized human agency, reform and change.[2] Thus, for example, the present inclusion of course material on multicultural education and sex equity in the social studies curricula of a number of school districts in this country (Swartz, 1989; Wisconsin Department of Public Instruction, 1986) has been in part the triumph of liberal interpretations of the more radical demands of subordinated minority and women's groups for drastic changes in the content of the school curriculum.[3] As I will show, these nuances and subtle differences within mainstream research frameworks are consequential not only in terms of theory, but also for the politics of pedagogical practices in education. As Nkomo (1984) and Sarup (1986) have argued, it is within the cracks and crevices of mainstream thought that a more radical discourse can be articulated.

Conservative Theories

These observations aside, mainstream theories of racial inequality in education rest squarely on particular conceptualizations of the nature and function of schooling in general. Thus, mainstream researchers have attempted to grasp the inner workings of American schools and their relationship to society in terms of psychometric frames of reference (Venn, 1984). This has involved a powerful consolidation and naturalization of methods of quantification and measurement, the predominance of positivistic empiricist approaches to the analysis of educational and social phenomena and the steady incorporation of mainstream research into establishment policies and agendas. Mainstream research has too often chosen a recourse to genetic epistemology, grounding its hypotheses and findings ultimately in biology and science (Henriques, 1984; Walkerdine, 1984). Its theories have usually cast the individual learner as the object of scientific/psychological inquiry (Walkerdine, 1984). For example, the insertion into curricular discourses of Piaget's conceptualization of the cognitive development of children in terms of 'developmental stages' has had the effect of a reification of these stages in the 'scope and sequence' of curriculum planning and the day-to-day pedagogical practices in schools (Walkerdine, 1984).

Against this background of the 'normative gaze' (West, 1982) of mainstream educational discourse, minority boys and girls have been construed as 'deviant' entities in educational and social arrangements.[4] Conventional mainstream educational research has stabilized a discourse around the 'deviance' of disadvantaged groups, using a variety of measures of difference, such as IQ tests calibrated on the normative performance of middle-class white males. Having arrived at these measures of individual differences, mainstream researchers have then turned around and typecast whole social groups (Carby, 1982). Early race and sex relations theorists, Galton, Gobineau and Hall, argued that genetic differences constituted indelible markers of the relative capacities of different groups of human beings. These genetic differences were conceptualized as determining the hierarchy of classes and races and men's superiority over women (Gould, 1981; Mullard, 1985; Selden, 1985, 1988). On the terrain of curriculum and educational theory and practice, Bobbit, Charters, Goddard, Snedden and Thorndike — proponents of mental tesing, social efficiency and scientific management — went somewhat further, and argued that minorities and immigrant women and men were a threat to the social order (Apple, 1979; Kliebard, 1986). Besides making arguments for the technical rationalization and efficiency of classroom pedagogy and school curriculum organization, these conservative educators maintained that controlled breeding (eugenics) should complement mental testing as a means of scientifically regulating the numbers and social effects of the low-ability progeny of the socially disadvantaged (Selden, 1985).

Though there are certain totalizing tendencies in the way in which conservative mainstream theorists (both past and present) have specified the relationship of educability to biology, there are contradictions within these frameworks. That is to say that though conservative educators reference racial, class and sexual phenomena within a common ground of biology and science, this floor of 'commonsense' is manipulated in uneven, discontinuous and contradictory ways. As an explanatory variable, biology is often mobilized very differently in conservative accounts of racial differences than in regard to, say, gender differences in school performance. For example, the theme of 'minority failure in schooling' was (is) construed in conservative mainstream frameworks in terms of a particular narrative that assembled biological/scientific data to flesh out a story of 'original loss'. Racial minorities were construed as having a unique location within the evolutionary process of humankind (Gobineau, 1915; Spencer, 1892). Thus, early twentieth-century curriculum planners advocated the radical differentiation of the school curriculum (Apple, 1979). According to these conservative educators, minority youth should be given a special type of education in keeping with their inferior mental abilities and their likely occupational destination in the secondary labor market. Lewis Terman (1916) made an especially strident case for the racial stratification of the curriculum based on inherited differences. For Terman, a special curriculum needed to be organized that would take full account of the special liabilities and needs of African Americans, Mexicans and Native Americans who, he maintained, were intellectually inferior to white people:

Their dullness seems racial, or at least inherent in the family stocks from which they come. The fact that one meets this type with such extraordinary frequency among Indians, Mexicans, and Negroes suggests quite forcibly that the whole question of racial differences in mental traits will have to be taken up anew ... There will be discovered enormously significant differences ... which can not be wiped out by any schemes of mental culture. Children of this group should be segregated in special classes. They cannot master abstractions but they can often be made efficient workers. (pp. 27–28)

On the other hand, the differential educability of girls and young women was (is) lodged more directly in a biological/sexual narrative that distinguished women's biological and, hence, social functions, capacities and orientation from those of men (Elshtain, 1986). It was their sex/gender inscription as 'feminine', as prospective procreators, as 'mothers', and so forth, that constituted young women's chief liability educationally and determined the need for a separate curriculum.[5] As Kliebard (1986) tells us, early twentieth-century American educators such as Hall 'advocated special versions of botany, biology, and chemistry designed for girls' and strongly recommended sex segregation in schooling (p. 48).

Within the past few years, there has been a resurgence of biological determinism (*Newsweek*, 30 May 1988; Selden, 1988). Writers such as Dunn (1987), Jensen (1981, 1984) and Loehlin, Linzey and Spuhler (1975) have strongly reasserted the claim that certain ethnic groups lack either the appropriate mental structures or the genetic make-up (in the 1920s and the 1930s, the heyday of Wiggam, Goddard, and Terman, it would have been 'germ cells') for high-level cognitive or intellectual tasks. Thus, 'they are incapable of achieving to the extent of whites' (Sue and Padilla, 1986, p. 43). I will not discuss this literature in any detail here. There are substantial and thorough refutations of biological determinism elsewhere (Gould, 1981; Ogbu, 1978; Selden, 1985, 1988; Sowell, 1977). Suffice it to say that critics have pointed to a number of conceptual and methodological problems associated with biological explanations of educational differences, particularly with respect to the work of Eysenck and Jensen. Among these criticisms are the following:

1   Intelligence tests, the principal quantitative instrument used by biological determinists to predict cognitive capacity, are hopelessly flawed in that such tests are culturally biased to the

advantage of Anglos and whites. In addition, liberal educators and cognitive psychologists such as Stodolsky and Lesser (1967) and Gardner (1984) have argued that the 'demonstration of intelligence' is a contextual and variable phenomenon. Intelligence is not, they maintain, an 'essence' or a 'deposit' that is 'measurable' in any simple or indisputable way.

2 Serious methodological errors result from attempts to define human groups as unitary or discrete biological entities of 'races'. As Troyna and Williams (1986), West (1988) and others have argued, 'races' are social entities — the products of historical, cultural and political struggles and forces rather than biological or genetic endowments. The concept 'white' used to define Americans with European ancestry, for example, artificially homogenizes erstwhile heterogeneous groups of Euro-American peoples who can lay claim to a plurality of 'origins'.

3 Proponents of biological explanations of educational differences such as Eysenck and Kamin (1981) and Jensen (1969, 1981, 1984) continue to draw heavily on the earlier work of differential psychologists such as Terman, Goddard and Burt — work which has been significantly discredited because of highly subjective manipulation of data and numerous statistical distortions (Ogbu, 1978).[6]

In a general sense, then, mainstream conservative accounts which rely on biological explanations of racial inequality in schooling are ahistorical and unreflexive. Over the history of mental testing, eugenics, differential psychology and social efficiency in curriculum planning in the United States, many immigrant and minority groups have been designated as genetically inferior. Indeed, the early research on IQ tests found differences between Southern and Eastern European immigrants and the majority populations similar to those found today between blacks and whites. Hurn (1979) draws attention to the historical variability of immigrant/minority performance on IQ tests:

Among the many objections that can be made to these assertions, the historical data on the test scores of immigrant groups are perhaps the most decisive ... Thomas Sowell has shown that many immigrant groups showed performance patterns on IQ tests similar to those of contemporary black students. A survey of Italian American mental scores administered shortly after World War I, for example, showed an average IQ of below 84 ... A contemporary study in Massachusetts showed a higher percentage of black students with IQ scores over 120 than Portuguese, Italian or French Canadian students ... In contrast to their consistent superiority on tests of verbal ability in recent times, in a 1921 study that Sowell reports, Jews exceeded all other immigrant groups in the 'number of certificates for mental defect' at Ellis Island. (p. 131)

Despite the historical evidence and the other limitations I have mentioned, a commonsense view that insists that minorities are mentally inferior to whites still prevails in some conservative mainstream accounts of racial inequality in schooling (Dunn, 1987). The adoption of a 'biological perspective' by these educators has led to the advocacy of curriculum and educational policies which emphasize social control and regulation of minority youth. In the past, conservative educators such as Hall, Snedden and Ross have advocated that minority and immigrant youth should be segregated in their own classes, or prohibited from public education altogether because of presumed 'intellectual limitations' (Ogbu, 1978; Ogbu and Matute-Bianchi, 1986). More contemporary thinkers like Jensen (1969, 1981, 1984) recommend a separate curriculum for minority students that would emphasize vocational studies rather than abstract academic subject matter (Ogbu, 1978; Ogbu and Matute-Bianchi, 1986).

As Gould (1981) reminds us, 'biological determinism is in its essence, a theory of limits' (p. 28). It is this sense of 'limits' that informs the intellectual cynicism that underscores conservative thinking on race and education. Conservative advocates of biological explanations of educational differences suggest that little can be done to remove or assuage the achievement differences between minority and majority groups. Educators and curriculum practitioners must content themselves with the fact that they can only help minority youth to 'meet whatever potentials are dictated by nature' (Sue and Padilla, 1986, p. 43).

New Conservative Perspectives on Race and Education

The biological determinism of Jensen and others therefore represents a certain continuity with a racial theme that had preoccupied later nineteenth- and early twentieth-century educational and social theorists: that the inferior capacities of minorities, particularly blacks and

Native Americans, explain their underachievement in intellectual and social life. The idea that genetic or biological differences explain racial differences in social and educational achievement is, regrettably, still alive and well within the popular consciousness in the United States. Indeed, a recent survey of 2,100 college students at forty-one campuses across the country found, among other things, that 'forty-five percent of the students [believe] that some races are more "evolved" than others' (*Newsweek*, 30 May 1988, p. 59).

However, within the last decade or so, some conservative educators and social theorists have introduced new and powerful inflections to traditional biological perspectives on racial inequality. Proponents of neo-conservative approaches to race and education such as Bloom (1987), Loury (1985), Steele (1989) and Sowell (1981), have sought to rearticulate traditional conservative discourses over social control and efficiency to more cultural and attitudinal explanations of minority failure. At the same time, neo-conservative educators have effectively rearticulated liberal concerns with equality of opportunity to more conservative themes of 'individual responsibility', 'individual effort', and the need to build a 'color-blind society'. For example, Shelby Steele (1989) maintains in a recent article that minority underachievement and low rates of graduation from major universities in the United States have more to do with the deep sense of intellectual and cultural inferiority that individual blacks feel in the presence of whites and less to do with the resurgence of campus racism, as black students and others have charged. For Steele, then, black students displace their anxiety over their own abilities and competence to the university system as a whole, choosing political grandstanding and protest rather than confronting the academic challenges that being at a major university presents. Steele (1989) argues provocatively:

> Denial [of the complex of self-doubt and insecurity that black students feel], and the distortion that results, places the problem outside the self and in the world. It is not that I have any inferiority anxiety because of my race; it is that I am going to school with people who don't like blacks. This is the shift in thinking that allows black students to reenact the protest pattern of the sixties. Denied racial anxiety-distortion-reenactment is the process by which feelings of inferiority are transformed into an exaggerated white menace — which is then protested against with the techniques of the past. Under the sway of this process, black students believe that history is repeating itself, that it's just like the sixties, or fifties. In fact, it

is the not yet healed wounds from the past, rather than the inequality that created the wounds, that is the real problem. This process generates an unconscious need to exaggerate the level of racism on campus — to make it a matter of the system, not just a handful of students. Racism is the avenue away from the true inner anxiety. How many students demonstrating for a black 'theme house' ... might be better off spending their time reading and studying? (p. 51).

Because many of these neo-conservative writers such as Steele directly address issues of educational policy and social agenda setting, I will defer a more substantive discussion of their perspectives until Chapter 6. In that chapter, I will explicitly address issues of educational practice and race relations reform. Here, it is enough to say that neo-conservative writers hold minorities up to severe and relentless cultural scrutiny (Hunter, 1986). They suggest that it is 'negative attitudes' and cultural deviance among minorities themselves that explain their lack of success in education and society. (According to Loury, 'There are deep structural problems within black communities having to do with values and attitudes', quoted in Simpson, 1987, p. 164.) Interestingly, these rather severe cultural evaluations of minorities are advanced by both black and white neo-conservatives. For instance, some black writers such as Sowell (1981) suggest that historical patterns of slave plantation paternalism and present-day state welfarism and trusteeship have helped to spawn a culture of clientelism and dependency among minority underclasses. These writers also maintain that liberals have unnecessarily politicized issues concerning ethnicity — often to the detriment of minorities themselves.

Ultimately, neo-conservatives suggest that tendencies toward cultural exceptionalism and cultural deviance among minorities should not be encouraged either in educational institutions or in society ('I think universities should emphasize a higher value than "diversity" and "pluralism" — buzzwords for the politics of difference', Steele, 1989, p. 55). They feel that the cultural incorporation and 'productive' participation of minorities in the dominant society are highly desirable social goals not only for the general economic health of American society, but for minorities themselves — large numbers of whom now lack the skills to participate in education and in the economy on equal terms with whites. For according to Patterson:

Industrialized civilization [imposes] a growing cultural and structural complexity which requires persons to have a broad grasp of what Professor Hirsch has called cultural literacy: a deep understanding of mainstream culture, which no longer has much to do with Anglo-Saxon Protestants, but with the imperatives of industrial civilization. It is the need for cultural literacy, a profound conception of the whole civilization, which is often neglected in talk about literacy. (quoted in Hirsch, 1987, p. 10)

We will meet Professor Patterson again in Chapter 6.

Liberal Theories

Conservative and neo-conservative formulations on these and other matters do not tell the full story of mainstream accounts of education. Liberal curriculum and educational theories represent a major inflection on mainstream accounts of racial inequality taken as a whole. They affirm the heterogeneous origins of the American populace and emphasize the plural character of American society (Davis and Moore, 1945; Easton, 1965; Glazer and Moynihan, 1963; Hurn, 1979). In these accounts, American schools comprise one set of institutions in a plurality of consensus-making social institutions through which various competing social groups seek to articulate their needs and interests. These social groups are conceptualized in terms of aggregates of individuals. A set of economic indicators, mainly occupational status, defines social class (SES). Cultural and biological indicators such as ancestry, national/religious affinity and physical/sexual traits are the bases on which liberal thinkers designate the social identities of minorities and women. However, unlike their more conservative colleagues, liberal school critics have sought to avoid 'innateness' and biological characteristics pure and simple as the bases for making causal inferences about socially disadvantaged groups. Though they also avoid the more negative and pessimistic assessments of minority culture associated with the neo-conservatives, liberal school critics have placed enormous emphasis on patterns in the social environment and culture of both minorities and majority peoples in their explanations of social and economic inequalities among different racial groups.

Just before and just after World War II, the social psychological writings of Adorno, Frenkel-Brunswik, Levinson and Sanford (1950), Allport (1954), Myrdal (1944) and Thomas (1928) set the liberal tone for the theorization and empirical investigation of factors underlying social inequality in American society. These writers drew attention to the attitudes, values and beliefs of dominant white society which served to delegitimate and undermine the social/psychological status and life chances of members of working-class and minority groups. But like mainstream conservative theories of racial inequality, these liberal accounts displayed certain tensions with respect to the individual versus society dualism. Though prejudice of all forms derived from consensual values in the dominant society, it was the individual, argued Adorno et al. (1950) and Allport (1954), who was the vehicle for acts of racism and prejudice.

Myrdal (1944) and Adorno et al. (1950) drew attention to the consensual respect for democratic values that existed in civilized western societies like the United States. Their negative grid points of reference were the fascism of Hitlerite Germany and the 'totalitarianism' of the communist USSR. Myrdal agonized over the 'dilemma' that he saw in American society. On the one hand, dominant white American society universally respected the principle of equality of opportunity, but at the same time, white Americans denied equality of status to the minority black population. Neo-classical economic theory and the status attainment formulations of Becker (1957), Friedman (1962) and Arrow (1973) associated racism with a certain 'taste for discrimination' expressed by agents operating in the market. Microeconomic theory, like neo-classical sociology, held a fundamental faith in the regulatory power and rationality of freely competitve capitalism to liquidate the contaminating effects of atavistic ethnic and sexual particularism in the marketplace (Reich, 1981, pp. 76–108). Henriques (1984) identifies two premises common to these social psychological and classical economic approaches to racism and social prejudice: (a) 'the belief in rationality as an ideal for a democratic society', and (b) the emphasis on the 'individual as the site of the breakdown of this rationality and therefore the object of research' (p. 66).

On the terrain of educational theory specifically, liberal thinkers also cast the issue of racial inequality in terms of the individual versus society dualism. However, most liberal theorists approached the subject of racial inequality through the 'SES paradigm' (Omi and Winant, 1986, pp. 25–38). In the 1960s, argues Hurn (1979), sociologists of education sought to test 'the meritocratic hypothesis' (p. 88). The work of researchers such as Duncan, Featherstone and Duncan (1972), Sewell and Hauser (1975) and Jencks (1972) attempted to connect the issue of unequal school performance with 'unequal social context' (Whitty, 1985). These researchers often combined a strong theoretical disposition towards a radical structural functionalism with highly sophisticated, empirically-based analyses of education. Their works tended to follow one of two paths: (a) highly quantitative studies which focused on extra-school explanations (SES, ethnicity, etc.) of educational failure (Coleman, 1966; Jencks, 1972; Sexton, 1961), or (b) qualitative studies which dealt with in-school explanations of unequal school performance (Cicourel and Kitsuse, 1963; Rist, 1970). In a significant work which focused on class and intergenerational mobility, Blau and Duncan (1967) used SES data compiled in a large national sample of males, taken from the 1960 US census, to compute the relationship between father's and son's status over time. After controlling for the effects of the expansion of higher status occupations in the society as a whole, they came to the conclusion that there had been no significant change between 1920 and 1960 in intergenerational mobility patterns. (Similar conclusions would be drawn with respect to race and intergenerational mobility, Ogbu, 1978.)

The work of Jencks (1972) and Coleman (1966) looked at the relationship of school resources to equality of opportunity. These writers concluded that the former had little or no effect on the latter. They maintained that inequality was generated elsewhere in the social and economic environment of socially disadvantaged minority youth. Thus according to Spring (1985), 'Both the Jencks study and the Coleman Report suggested that the inequalities in educational opportunity have very little effect on educational attainment and, consequently, on intergenerational mobility' (p. 78). Liberal theorists revisited, assessed and ultimately rejected the connections between IQ test scores and school outcomes made by past and present conservative theorists such as Jensen (1969, 1981). Hurn (1979), for example, maintained that 'we must reject the hypothesis of distinctive patterns of performance among the black populations' (p. 132).

However, while rejecting conservative emphasis on the defective innate capacities of children from minority and low socioeconomic groups, some liberal educators sought to explain minority failure by an equally damning theory. These educators claimed that minority youth were 'culturally deprived' (Ausubel, 1964; Bloom, Davis and Hess, 1965; Gottfried, 1973; Hunt, 1964). According to this theory, children are culturally deprived when they come from home environments that do not provide the kind of organized stimulation that fosters 'normal' development. As a consequence, 'they are retarded in linguistic, cognitive, and social development, which is why they fail in school' (Ogbu, 1978, p. 44). The explanation of educational differences in terms of minority 'cultural deficits' was given added credence by the findings of the Columbia University Work Conference on Curriculum and Teaching in Depressed Urban Areas in 1962, the Chicago Conference on Compensatory Education for the Culturally Deprived in 1964 and individual liberal scholars such as Bloom, Davis and Hess (1965), Brooks (1966) and Moynihan (1965). Bloom, Davis and Hess, in their volume, *Compensatory Education for Cultural Deprivation*, defined culturally deprived students in the following terms:

> In the present educational system in the United States (and elsewhere) we find a substantial group of students who do not make normal progress in their school learning. Predominantly, these are students whose early experiences in the home, whose motivation for school learning, and whose goals for the future are such as to handicap them in their school work. (1965, p. 4)

Researchers such as Rist (1970), Rosenthal and Jacobson (1968) and Cicourel and Kitsuse (1963) pointed in a somewhat different direction — to the internal school culture and the pedagogical practices of teachers and their interpretations and expectations for socially disadvantaged minority youth. Among these qualitative and ethnographic investigations of classroom life, the work of Ray Rist (1970) stands out as being particularly significant. In his study of an all-black elementary school in St. Louis, Rist found that the kindergarten teacher assigned the children in her classroom to three different ability groups from the first week of their arrival. These ability groups were established on the basis of criteria (skin color, dress and parental background) which correlated strongly with socioeconomic status. (The powerful intra-racial implications of these dynamics were not comprehensively taken up by Rist, but are clearly deducible from the qualitative data provided.) Original tracks of 'most promising', 'promising' and 'least promising', assigned by the teacher on the eighth day after the children first arrived at the school were 'caste-like' in that there was little or no mobility between the tracks over the course of the school year. Rist contends that the children internalized these labels established by the external authority of the teacher. This tracking process, instituted so early in the school lives of these students, constituted a self-fulfilling prophecy which they would live out the rest of their school careers.

In recent years, liberal researchers such as Heath (1986), Ogbu and Matute-Bianchi (1986) and Sue and Padilla (1986) have authored sophisticated theoretical and anthrophological studies that have gone somewhat beyond the earlier work of Rist (1970) in exploring the relationship between student-teacher interaction and minority dispositions toward schooling and academic success. These researchers contend that minority students' perceptions of teacher behavior — what Heath (1986) calls 'cultural learning' — are as crucial as teacher expectations in determining minority school outcomes. Of these writers, Ogbu (1978) and Ogbu and Matute-Bianchi (1986) have gone the furthest towards elaborating a conceptual framework which links student-teacher interaction over differences in academic achievement in the classroom to larger sociocultural forces beyond the school. In their conceptual framework, Ogbu and Matute-Bianchi (1986) emphasize the following: (a) minority school performance is a variable phenomenon, not only in the United States but in other countries (for instance, Chinese Americans are generally successful in American schools, Mexican Americans are not; West Indian youth do better in schools in the United States than West Indian youth do in English schools); (b) schools are linked to larger historical forces and socioeconomic systems, particularly the job market; and (c) the relationship between school and the job market (as expressed in the type of job opportunities available to minorities) influences minority youth perceptions of the school's ability to help them 'get ahead in the United States society' (Ogbu and Matute-Bianchi, 1986, p. 73). Specifically, they argue that, primarily through functional adaptation over time to sociocultural and economic circumstances, different minority groups develop different 'status mobility systems' or 'folk theories of getting ahead' (Ogbu and Matute-Bianchi, 1986). Simply put, some groups (autonomous or immigrant minorities — Chinese Americans) develop folk theories which 'enhance their ability in schools', while other groups (caste-like minorities — Mexicans and black Americans) develop folk theories which 'limit their school achievement capacity' (Cortes, 1986, p. 25).

Distinctions can be drawn between Ogbu and Matute-Bianchi's (1986) research on minority underachievement and earlier qualitative research that attempted to address the subject. On the whole, liberal qualitative research and teacher expectations studies of Rist (1970), Rosenthal and Jacobson (1968) and others blame teachers for minority and working-class underachievement. They maintain that teachers' interpretations of dress, demeanor and speech of minority and working-class youth profoundly influence the disproportionate assignment of these disadvantaged youth to lower ability groups and tracks. The recent work of Ogbu and Matute-Bianchi (1986) and Heath (1986) turns this thesis around by suggesting that it is student perceptions of teacher behavior as well as the limited job opportunities that historically have been made available to black and other 'caste-like' minority youth that determine the latter's devaluation of academic success.

Though in significant ways writers such as Ogbu and Matute-Bianchi strain their relationship with liberal mainstream research on educational differences by pointing to the powerful effects of 'socio-economic system' such as the job market, much of their conceptual framework on racial inequality in schooling still rests firmly on mainstream educational and race relations theories that privilege 'values', 'attitudes' and 'opportunity'. Since, in a general sense, liberal research on racial inequality lacks a theory of power, it is not clear what motivates certain attitudes and what types of organizational assets and capacities influence unequal educational outcomes. The problem of unequal race relations in schooling is therefore depoliticized and reduced to a much more narrow educational and professional language or 'non-racist' discourse over what facilitates or obstructs minority achievement in the classroom (Brown, 1985).

Liberal Discourses and Educational Policy

Probably the most compelling feature of this liberal research on race and education, as Berlowitz (1984) has pointed out, has been its impact on the shaping of educational policy discourses in the United States. The power of liberal positions on education and social inequality, argues one school critic, resides in their hegemonic connections to establishment discourses. As 'policy intellectuals' (Berlowitz, 1984, p. 129), liberal educators can exploit the strategic interface of their work with agendas of the state. It is, however, somewhat simplistic to maintain, as writers such as Berlowitz (1984) and Edari (1984) have, that liberal research is unproblematically incorporated into establishment frameworks. There are, for example, radical and fragmentary moments, tensions and breaks which systematically inform the relationship between liberal scholarship and establishment agendas (Wexler, 1976). These tensions exist even when liberal formulations retain a linguistic and instrumental affinity to establishment discourses. In a general sense, then, liberal theories and programs directed at educational differences in schooling could be described as 'progressive' or 'possibilitarian' — when contrasted with conservative agendas.

In the last three decades or so, following upon the demands of the protest and civil rights movements of the 1950s and 1960s and the impact of the radical ideas of minority school critics, liberal educators and policy makers in the United States pushed forward (by fits and starts) an active program of ameliorative reforms directed at improving the educational performance of minority and socially disadvantaged youth. The liberal approach to school inequality was fundamentally integrationist. The most visible aspect of this integrationist agenda was embodied in the drive for school desegregation across the country — an initiative directly precipitated by the Supreme Court desegregation order of 1954. The curricular and pedagogical component of this liberal integrationist strategy took the form of compensatory programs such as Operation Head Start, Follow Through and Upward Bound, administered by the Office for Economic Opportunity, and remedial education projects provided for under Title I of the Elementary and Secondary Education Act (ESEA) of 1965. These compensatory and remedial programs were directly influenced by the cultural deprivation hypotheses of liberal theorists such as Bloom, Davis and Hess (1965). These programs were largely designed to make up for the sociocultural 'deficits' that presumably caused minority children to fail. Black and Hispanic youth were to be in some sense redeemed from the influences of their home and neighborhood environments 'by resocializing them to develop those skills essential for success in the public schools: language or communication skills, reasoning ability, motivation, pride in achievement, perceptual skills, long attention span, and feeling of self-worth' (Ogbu, 1978, p. 84).

The educational results of these integrationist educational policies have been mixed. It seems once again that the problem of racial inequality was misdiagnosed. On the one hand, the policy of school segregation met and continues to meet with considerable white resistance (Smith, 1988). On the other hand, compensatory and remedial education programs such as Operation Head Start, Follow Through and Upward Bound have not produced the kind of sustained or long-term boost to the academic performance of black and Hispanic students that had been anticipated by liberal reformers (*Education Week*, 14 May, 1986; Ogbu and Matute-Bianchi, 1986; Pettigrew, 1969).

These harsh facts have helped to fuel a certain pessimism within public and academic circles toward liberal policies of integration and educational compensation. Some black sociologists of education such as Ogbu (1978) have been particularly critical. While acknowledging that minority families and children involved in compensatory education programs have benefited from ancillary services, Ogbu argues that programs like Head Start have failed to deliver on their primary objective: closing the gap which currently exists between black and white children in educational achievement.[7] Drawing on the data from a 1965 national study of the impact of the Head Start program on minority school performance conducted by Westinghouse/Ohio University researchers, Ogbu (1978) maintains the following:

> The [Westinghouse/Ohio University] study examined the effects of both the summer and full-year Head Start program. In general, it was found that the summer program had no positive effects . . . The effect of the full-year program, though statistically significant, was not enough 'to make one believe that the child's academic prospects were improved' . . . In general, even the full-year Head Start program had not closed the gap in school performance between the advantaged and disadvantaged groups of students. For instance, children who had experienced a full year of Head Start training were about eight months behind the national norm on the Illinois Test of Psycholinguistic Abilities, and at about the forty-fourth percentile on the second grade Stanford–Binet Achievement test. (pp. 92–3)

It should be pointed out that not all liberal educators agree with Ogbu's negative assessment of compensatory education, and recent studies have been pointing to more positive results of programs such as Head Start. For example, in a recent volume, *Choosing Equality*, Bastian, Fruchter, Gittel, Greer and Haskins (1986) contend that compensatory education programs, particularly Head Start, have been modestly successful in closing some of the gaps in educational achievement that exist between minority and majority students. However, these authors suggest that the effectiveness of these programs was systematically undermined in the 1980s by drastic reduction in commitments and investments on the part of the federal government:

> In 1980, only 57 per cent of the approximately 9 million students eligible for Title I were provided compensatory services, even though recent studies indicate the program has produced measurable gains for recipients. By 1982, it was estimated that Title I reductions had cut 900,000 children out of the program. In 1980, 77 per cent of Hispanic children with limited English proficiency were not receiving any form of special programming responsive to their linguistic needs, only 10 per cent were in bilingual programs . . . Even the most

successful of the '60s programs, Head Start, which operates independently and innovatively with a record of unparalleled benefit for low-income children and their communities, today reaches only 18 per cent of all eligible children. (Bastian *et al.*, 1986, p. 46)

These observations on compensatory education aside, there are significant conceptual problems that ultimately limit the effectiveness of liberal strategies and approaches to racial inequality and educational differences taken as a whole. Mainstream theorists tend to see the institutional life of American society in atomistic and restrictive terms. Education is therefore largely conceptualized as separate and detached from the political and economic life of society. When connections are made — as, for example, between education and the economy — the focus is not on systematic relations but on more restrictive concerns with empirical correlations between educational attainment and income differentials and on changing attitudes, not structures. In this sense, the theories of cultural deprivation which inform liberal policies of compensatory education reduce the problem of racial inequality and the attendant socioeconomic disadvantage that minority youth face to the more innocuous discourse of school readiness and minority academic performance pure and simple. If only practitioners could help boost the academic performance of subordinated minority youth, black students could pull even with their white counterparts. The future of the former would be secure. The problems associated with racial inequality would go away.

More broadly, within mainstream frameworks, education is seen in the limited sense as the acquisition of skills and competencies in preparation for the assumption of adult responsibilities in working life. Education is not seen as a site of the production of racial differences. Thus, for example, proponents of school integration have concentrated almost exclusively on numbers, quotas, ratios and so forth in their drive to desegregate the schools. The need to actively promote positive race relations in American schools has not been emphasized (Kagan, 1986).

Finally, liberal accounts of education are overwhelmingly psychologistic and focus on individual differences. Such an emphasis has tended to vitiate the power of liberal analysis with respect to the nature and effects of raced, classed and gendered collectivities. It is this very emphasis on the 'unattached individual' and the inability to take seriously the truly structural relationship that exists between schooling and race, gender and class dynamics that ultimately undermines the

Figure 2.1   Typology of mainstream curriculum accounts of race

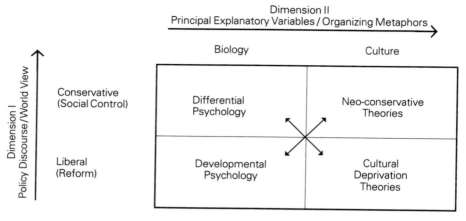

progressive potential of liberal mainstream approaches to racial in-equality in schooling.

Conclusion

In this chapter, I have discussed the strengths and weaknesses of the mainstream literature on racial inequality in schooling in some detail. Particular attention was paid to the tensions and discontinuities be-tween conservative and liberal mainstream approaches to the race/education couplet. I suggested that there were two principal tensions or contradictions in the mainstream accounts of racial inequality in schooling. First, a tension between control and reform (Dimension I) is expressed in conservative versus liberal policy discourses and world views on education and society. Second, a tension between biology and culture (Dimension II) exists both within conservative theories themselves and between conservative theories and liberal explanations of racial differences in education. These tensions or contradictions are summarized in Figure 2.1.

As we saw, mainstream conservative curriculum theorists from Hall (1904) to Jensen (1981) have attempted to explain racial inequality in schooling by means of a genetic hypothesis. In these accounts, minority genetic inferiority explains the failure of minority youth in school. Racial inequality results from the failure of minority youth to secure the type of academic credentials that would guarantee social status and social rewards. Conservative emphasis on biological explanations of racial and educational differences are usually accompanied by a pessimistic policy discourse of social regulation and control (Ogbu, 1978; Sue and Padilla, 1986). As I also emphasized, not all conservatives espouse biological determinism. Neo-conservatives such as Bloom (1987), Sowell (1981) and Steele (1989) point to minority cultural deviance and negative attitudes toward self and work as the primary causes of minority educational failure.

While liberal educators also 'blame the victim', these educators do take a distinctly non-biological view of racial differences and minority underachievement. They also avoid some of the more severe evaluations and conclusions about minority culture offered in neo-conservative discussions of racial differences in education. Curriculum theorists such as Bloom, Davis and Hess (1965), Bell (1975) and Orr (1987) suggest that minorities fail because of their lack of access in the home to the cultural and intellectual resources that are available to white middle-class youth. Liberal educators have therefore contended that compensatory forms of education would ameliorate minority cultural deficits and hence remove the primary obstacles to minority educational and social success.

As I indicated earlier, curricular policies predicated on these mainstream positions have not been successful in eliminating differentials in minority and majority educational performance or job chances beyond the school. While these liberal approaches and the programs they have engendered have a great deal of merit, as I will argue in Chapter 6, a broader critique of the state and education is required as the basis of the struggle for race-relations reform. In significant ways, then, the problem of racial inequality in schooling has been inadequately theorized within mainstream frameworks. It is in the context of the failure of mainstream approaches to racial inequality, and the persistent evidence of minority underachievement and growing disenchantment with the school curriculum, that liberal educators (particularly black scholars) forged a new discourse of cultural emancipation or multiculturalism in the 1970s. In the next chapter, I will discuss the discursive origins and development of the multicultural agenda in American schools.

Notes

1   Poster (1984) quite succinctly paraphrases Foucault's claim with respect to the relationship of the social sciences to systems of control and social regulation. Foucault's argument, Poster contends, is that 'The disciplines

which take "man" [sic] as their object also have "man" [sic] as their subject. The hermeneutic circle produces a certain blindness which allows the human sciences to avoid reflecting upon their effects on practice' (p. 86). Critical curriculum theorists have also argued against the notion that knowledge is unmediated. They insist that knowledge is itself a site of domination and struggle (Wexler, 1982, 1987).

2 Wexler (1976) makes the very useful observation that mainstream research is characterized by genuinely conservative and progressive tensions. He argues that these 'progressive possibilitarian' and conservative moments are dynamically related and can be seen at times to commingle in a single curricular discourse. For example, the discourse of 'scientific efficiency' which emerged in early twentieth-century curriculum planning in the United States provided liberals and progressive educators with powerful conceptual and methodological tools which helped to debunk oppressive pedagogical practices in the classroom and an elitist curriculum emphasis on the classics, mental discipline and so on. But at the same time, it was the discourse of utilitarian science which actively informed the eugenics movement. Advocates of scientific efficiency, such as Charters (1926), sought to introduce new managerial controls on the classroom teacher. These utilitarian educators joined with dominant interest groups in pursuing a ruthless quest for standardization and technical rationalization of the school curriculum.

3 Under the subheading 'Equity and Curriculum', the writers of the State of Wisconsin DPI's *A Guide to Curriculum Planning in Social Studies* (1986) maintain the following:

> The state and the nation recognize the differences in the experiences of women and men of all races, colors, ethnic groups, and people of varied physical and mental abilities. These factors often result in the sorting, grouping, and tracking, of female, minority, and disabled students in stereotyped patterns that prevent them from exploring all options and opportunities according to their individual talents and interests. The cost of bias to academic achievements, psychological and physical development, careers, and family relationships is significant. All students should have the opportunity to observe their own places in the curriculum, to grow and develop, and to attain identity. (p. xi)

Even though this approach to social equity situates the issue of unequal opportunities and rewards in individual differences, interests and so forth, the language is clearly ameliorative.

4 West (1982), drawing on the writings of Foucault (1970), situates the language of 'deviance' and the epistemology of difference in the genealogy of racism. He locates racial categories in the origins and elaboration of a positivist scientific method that emerged in the sixteenth and seventeenth centuries. Such empiricist science placed an enormous emphasis on 'measurement', 'observation', 'comparison' and their anthropological and sociological derivative — the 'normative gaze'. West (1982) asserts:

My argument is that the authority of science, undergirded by Greek ocular metaphors and Cartesian notions, promotes and encourages the activities of observing, comparing, measuring, and ordering the physical characteristics of human bodies ... The creative fusion of scientific investigation, Cartesian epistemology and classical ideals produced forms of rationality, scientificity, and objectivity which, though efficacious in the quest for the truth and knowledge, prohibited the intelligibility and legitimacy of black equality in beauty, culture, and intellectual capacity. In fact, to 'think' such an idea was to be deemed irrational, barbaric, or mad. (p. 48)

5   The particular narrative of gender differences associated with early curriculum theorists such as Hall and Charters involved the following claims: (a) real biological/sex differences were 'naturally' imposed or inscribed upon a generic human material from birth; (b) biological differences were seen as universal and immutable; and (c) these biological differences corresponded with certain differences in emotional and intellectual predisposition. Typically, girls and women were regarded as passive thinkers predisposed to the home, nurturing activities and so forth. Boys and men were seen as predisposed to be vigorously and ruthlessly competitive and intellectual in the stereotypical 'masculine' way.

6   See Ogbu (1978, p. 55) for an extended treatment of the methodological and theoretical 'problems' that he finds in the work of Jensen (1969) and other proponents of the genetic hypothesis.

7   Ogbu (1978, pp. 67–100) actually offers a very sensitive and trenchant discussion of the strengths and weaknesses of these compensatory education programs.

Chapter 3

The Multicultural Solution

Liberal compensatory education programs such as Head Start, discussed in Chapter 2, resulted from the collaboration of the state and liberal social science during the Kennedy and Johnson administrations of the 1960s (Banks, 1981). Multicultural education in turn emerged during this period in part as a minority response to the failure of these programs to address more fundamental demands for educational and social reform. At the same time, however, multicultural education was itself a direct consequence of the efforts of the state to redirect minority challenges to the persistence of racial inequality in American schools. Multiculturalism is therefore a product of a particular historical conjuncture of relations among the state, contending racial minority and majority groups, and policy intellectuals in the United States, at a time when the discourse over schools had become increasingly racialized. Black and other minority groups, for example, began to insist that curriculum and educational policy address issues of racial inequality, minority cultural identities and the distribution of power within institutions such as schools themselves (Banks, 1987; Berlowitz, 1984). Proponents of multiculturalism were very much influenced by these radical possibilitarian themes. But as we shall see, these educators often 'claw back' (Fiske and Hartley, 1978) from the radical themes associated with black challenges to the white-dominated school curriculum and school system.

This chapter will explore the theory and practice of multiculturalism as a contradictory and problematic 'solution' to racial inequality in schooling. First, I will outline the historical developments in American schooling and state policy toward racial minorities that led up to the events of the 1960s and the emergence of multiculturalism in education. Second, I will closely examine the general perspectives, core ideological assumptions and desired outcomes of three multicultural policy discourses on racial inequality in education. I will specifically look at the way these discourses are expressed in various school curriculum and preservice teacher education program guides as well as in the articulated theories of proponents of multicultural education. There are subtle differences among the policy discourses I will discuss that I will argue have important ideological and political implications.

Historical Background

For over one hundred years and up until two decades ago, a basic assimilationist model formed the centerpiece of education and state policies towards ethnic differences in the United States. Schooling was looked upon as the institution par excellence through which American educational policy-markers and ruling elites consciously attempted to cultivate norms of citizenship, to fashion a conformist American identity and to bind together a population of diverse national origins (Kaestle, 1983; Olneck and Lazerson, 1980). This assimilationist ideology was rooted in the nativistic response of dominant Northern Euro-Americans to the waves of immigrants from southern Europe who came to work in urban factories at the turn of the century. These southern European immigrants were seen as a threat to a social order that was based on the values of an earlier settled Euro-American citizenry. The latter traced their ancestry to England, the Netherlands and other northern European countries.

In 1909, Ellwood P. Cubberley, a proponent of 'social efficiency' (Kliebard, 1986, p. 223), clearly stated the case for using civil institutions such as schools as vehicles for cultivating dominant Anglo-Saxon values among the new immigrants and their offspring:

> Everywhere these people [immigrants] tend to settle in groups or settlements, and to set up here their national manners, customs, and observances. Our task is to break up these groups or settlements, to assimilate and amalgamate these people as part of our American race, and to implant in their children, as far as can be done, the Anglo-Saxon conception of righteousness, law and order, and popular government, and to awaken in them a reverence for our democratic institutions and for those things in our national life which we as a people hold to be of abiding truth. (Cubberley, 1909, pp. 15–16)

In addition to promoting highly conformist practices and values in schools, policy makers turned to the coercive apparatuses of the state to control the flow of non-Anglo immigrants into the United States. Highly exclusionary clauses were written into the United States Immigration Acts of 1917 and 1924 which drastically limited the number of immigrants who came from southern and eastern Europe, Asia and Latin America (Banks, 1981).

For American minority groups, institutional assimilationist practices were even more stringent and definitively conformist. Efforts were made in educational institutions serving Hispanic, Native American and black youth to rid these groups of 'ethnic traits' (Banks, 1981, p. 4) that were considered inimical to the dominant American culture. Consequently, early twentieth-century institutions such as the Hampton Institute were designed to equip black and Native American youth with 'the skills that would bring them to the level of the white middle class' (Kliebard, 1986, p. 126). The course in economics at Hampton, for example, 'attempted to get blacks and American Indians to abandon certain undesirable practices in specific areas of practical concern such as the purchase of clothing and the consumption of food' (Kliebard, 1986, p. 126).

For most of the first half of the century, this assimilationist model of education was not seriously challenged, even though black protest groups such as the United Negro Improvement Association, led by Marcus Garvey, championed separatism and pluralism. Indeed, many prominent black as well as white middle-class intellectuals regarded assimilation and cultural incorporation of American ethnic groups as a highly desirable social goal. In the 1920s and 1930s, the so-called Chicago School of sociologists, led by Robert E. Park (a former secretary to Booker T. Washington), outlined the basic assimilation model that was so influential in shaping research and social policy on race relations during the period. Park postulated that all immigrant and ethnic minority group members went through a 'race relations cycle' or trajectory on their way to eventual incorporation into the mainstream of American life. This cycle consisted of four stages: contact, conflict, accommodation and assimilation (Omi and Winant, 1986, p. 15).

But for minorities such as blacks and Native Americans, assimilation meant a special kind of cultural incorporation into a racial order in which they were accorded a secondary status. The ideology of assimilation clearly benefited white Americans. Over time, white 'ethnics' were able to share in the rewards of the society from which black Americans were systematically excluded. Blacks, Native

Americans and Hispanics continued to experience severe discrimination and racial exclusion in housing, employment and education during the first half of this century. During this same period, European immigrants — Irish, Italian and Greek — came, settled and consolidated their status in American society.

By the 1950s and 1960s, policies of assimilation had lost credibility among many minority groups and were subjected to unprecedented challenges by oppositional black groups and the civil rights movement. These challenges were particularly strong in the area of education. Black and other minority groups contended that schools as they were organized in America were fundamentally racist and did not address the needs and aspirations of minority peoples. Minority groups demanded more control of institutions in their communities. They demanded greater representation in the administration and staffing of schools. Even more significantly, black youth and their political leaders demanded a radical redefinition of the school curriculum to include Black Studies. The latter demand constituted a strategic challenge to the taken-for-granted Eurocentric foundations of the American school curriculum (McCarthy and Apple, 1988).

Essentially, then, the assimilationist approach to race relations and to the education of minorities had become unstuck. Blacks and other oppositional racial minorities had begun to champion a radical pluralism (Berlowitz, 1984). It was in this context of radical black discontent with American schooling that educational policy makers and liberal intellectuals began to forge a 'new' discourse of multiculturalism. Educators and social researchers such as Baker (1973), Banks (1973) and Glazer and Moynihan (1963) attempted to replace the assimilationist model that undergirded the American school curriculum with a pluralist model that embraced the notion of cultural diversity. Multicultural education as a 'new' curricular form disarticulated elements of black radical demands for the restructuring of school knowledge and rearticulated these elements into more reformist professional discourses around issues of minority failure, cultural characteristics and language proficiency.

Multicultural Policy Discourses

Over the years, policy discourses on multicultural education have consistently identified the variable of culture as the vehicle for the resolution of racial inequality and racial antagonism in schooling (Troyna and Williams, 1986). This central motif does represent a

certain continuity with an earlier emphasis on minority culture identifiable in the proposals of liberal scholars for compensatory education.
However, unlike the earlier liberal preoccupation with 'cultural deprivation', multicultural proponents have tended to emphasize the
positive qualities of minority cultural heritage. Proponents of multicultural education have therefore promoted curriculum models that
emphasize the following:

   a) *cultural understanding* — the idea central to many ethnic studies
       and human relations programs that students and teachers
       should be more sensitive to ethnic differences in the
       classroom;
   b) *cultural competence* — the insistence in bilingual and bicultural
       education programs that students and teachers should be able
       to demonstrate competence in the language and culture of
       groups outside their own cultural heritage; and
   c) *cultural emancipation* — the somewhat more possibilitarian and
       social-reconstructionist thesis that the incorporation/inclusion
       of minority culture in the school curriculum has the potential
       to influence minority academic achievement positively, and
       consequently to improve minority life chances beyond the
       school (Grant and Sleeter, 1989; Rushton, 1981).

   In the following sections, I will discuss in some detail the contradictions and nuances that are embodied in these three multicultural
approaches to racial inequality in education.

Models of Cultural Understanding

Models of cultural understanding in multicultural education exist in
the form of various state- and university-supported ethnic studies and
human relations programs which place a premium on 'improving
communication' among different ethnic groups (Montalto, 1981). The
fundamental stance of this approach to ethnic differences in schooling
is that of cultural relativism. Within this framework, all social and
ethnic groups are presumed to have a formal parity with each other.
The matter of ethnic identity is understood in terms of individual
choice and preference — the language of the shopping mall.
   This stance of cultural relativism is translated in curriculum
guides for ethnic studies in terms of a discourse of reciprocity and
consensus: 'We are different but we are all the same'. The idea that

racial differences are only 'human' and 'natural' is, for example, promoted in the teaching kit 'The Wonderful World of Difference: A Human Relations Program for Grades K-8', in which the authors 'explore the diversity and richness of the human family' (Anti-Defamation League of B'nai B'rith, 1986). In their *Multicultural Teaching: A Handbook of Activities, Information, and Resources*, Tiedt and Tiedt (1986) tell teachers and students that there are many different ways of grouping individuals in 'our society'. Income, religious beliefs and so on, are some of the criteria 'we use' in the United States. One of the handbook's many activities requires students to make up a list of cultural traits that would be characteristic of 'Sue Wong' (p. 144). Students are also asked to supply the appropriate cultural information that would help to complete the sentence 'Sue Wong is . . .' (p. 144). This tendency to focus on the acceptance and recognition of cultural differences has led in recent years to a movement for the recognition of the cultural 'uniqueness' of 'white ethnic' groups (for example, Poles, Italians, Norwegians and Swedes) to counterbalance demands for the study of black, Hispanic and Native American cultures (Gibson, 1984).

But the emphasis on cultural understanding goes beyond the development of communication skills and respect for ethnic differences. Various preservice teacher education programs and state human relations guides emphasize the elimination of racial and sexual stereotypes and the development of positive attitudes towards minority and disadvantaged groups (Wisconsin Department of Public Instruction, 1986). This emphasis on attitudinal change is, for example, reflected in the Ann Arbor, Michigan, Board of Education's regulations of the 1970s:

> Beginning in the 1972–73 school year, no student-teacher shall be accepted by the Ann Arbor schools unless he (she) can demonstrate attitudes necessary to support and create the multiethnic curriculum. Each student-teacher must provide a document or transcript which reflects training in or evidence of substantive understanding of multicultural or minority experience. (Baker, 1977, p. 80)

In a similar manner, the University of Winconsin-Madison Steering Committee on Minority Affairs, in its 1987 report, strongly emphasizes the need for course work that would promote racial tolerance:

The University must implement a mandatory six credit course requirement; and create and develop various Ethnic Studies Programs. These measures will recognize the contributions of ethnic minorities to American society and promote cross-cultural understanding and respect among the entire student body. (University of Wisconsin-Madison Steering Committee on Minority Affairs, p. 4)

Cultural understanding models of multicultural education, such as the one promoted in the University of Wisconsin-Madison Steering Committee on Minority Affairs report, generally take a 'benign' stance (Troyna and Williams, 1986) towards racial inequality in schooling and consequently place an enormous emphasis on promoting racial harmony among students and teachers from different cultural backgrounds. The following are some of the ideological assumptions that centrally inform this approach to racial differences in education:

a) The United States is a culturally and ethnically diverse nation;

b) This cultural diversity has had a positive effect on the overall growth and development of America as a powerful country (King, 1980; Tiedt and Tiedt, 1986);

c) All of America's ethnic groups have in their different ways contributed to the growth and development of America (Wisconsin Department of Public Instruction, 1986);

d) The educational system in the past has not sufficiently fostered this multicultural view of American society, and this has contributed to prejudice and discrimination against certain ethnic groups;

e) Schools and teachers must therefore positively endorse cultural diversity and foster an appreciation and respect for 'human differences' in order to reduce racial tension and estrangement of minority groups in the school and in society. (Tiedt and Tiedt, 1986)

The principal expectation of those who promote the cultural understanding model of multicultural education is that American schools will be oriented toward the 'cultural enrichment of all students' (Gibson, 1984, p. 99). It is assumed that teachers will provide such enrichment in their classrooms. By fostering understanding and acceptance of cultural differences in the classroom and in the school curriculum, it is expected that educational programs based on the cultural understanding approach will contribute toward the elimination of prejudice (Baker, 1977).

Proponents of this approach to multicultural education attach enormous significance to the role of attitudes in the reproduction of racism. Human relations and ethnic studies programs based on the cultural understanding model pursue what Banks (1981) calls the 'prejudiceless goal'. The strong version of these programs directly targets white students and teachers. White students and teachers are portrayed as the flawed protagonists in their racial relations with blacks and Native Americans. It is expected that negative white attitudes towards minorities will change if these prejudiced individuals are exposed to sensitivity training in human relations programs. The weak version of the cultural understanding approach emphasizes the promotion of racial harmony and tolerance of social and ethnic differences.

Various pretest/post-test evaluations of multicultural education and human relations programs that emphasize attitudinal change and cultural understanding suggest that these programs have not been very successful in achieving their espoused goal of eliminating majority/minority prejudice. For instance, although in her evaluation of the University of Michigan's human relations program Baker (1973) claims modest changes in white 'pro-irrational attitudes' (p. 307), these changes are not reported in the critical area of black/white relations. Thus, according to Baker, the Michigan students' perceptions of blacks remained at the 'pretest level' and were not significantly changed by the students' participation in the university's human relations program: 'No statistically significant differences obtained on the black anti-irrational or pro-irrational subscales. Therefore it can be concluded that the change in the perception of blacks held by the [white] students remained fairly constant' (p. 307).

Like Baker, Fish (1981) reports findings of 'no significant effects' in his study of the impact of the field experience component of Wisconsin's human relations program on white students' perceptions of blacks and other disadvantaged groups. According to Fish:

> Students who completed a fieldwork experience did not over a semester's time show significantly greater positive attitudes towards the population worked with than students who did not complete a fieldwork experience. (p. xi)

Indeed, Fish indicates a worsening of attitudes toward blacks during the course of the Wisconsin program:

> One semester after completion of a fieldwork experience, students' attitudes toward the mentally retarded and the physically disabled persisted at the pretest level, whereas students' attitudes toward blacks significantly worsened from the pretest level. (p. xii)

But Fish is not alone in his findings of unanticipated negative effects of attitudinal change programs. Buckingham (1984) draws similar conclusions in his case study of responses to 'The Whites of Their Eyes', a Thames Televsion educational program on 'Racism in the British Media'. In his study of the responses of 'a number of groups of London school pupils to the program', Buckingham drew the following conclusions:

> In general, for instance, pupils failed to perceive that the programme was concerned with racism in the media, and this led many to assume that the programme was suggesting that all white people are racist. Likewise few pupils picked up on the programme's arguments about the causes of racism, and fewer still seemed to have noticed its implicit suggestions about how racism might be eradicated. While the programme provides a fairly clear historical context for the discussion of racism, pupils generally failed to make connections between this and the examples of racism in the media today. (1984, p. 139)

American school critics have raised other concerns about attitudinal change and cultural understanding programs. Writers such as Pettigrew (1974) and Garcia (1974) have argued that the content and methods of these programs are significantly flawed. Pettigrew (1974), Garcia (1974) and Gibson (1984) point to the tendency of proponents of cultural understanding models to overemphasize the difference among ethnic groups, neglecting the differences within any one group. They also draw attention to the unintended effect of stereotyping which results from multicultural approaches that treat ethnic groups as 'monolithic entities possessing uniform, discernible traits' (Gibson, 1984, p. 100). For instance, Garcia contends that advocates of cultural understanding models tend to discuss 'Chicano culture as if it were a set of values and customs possessed by all who are categorized as Chicanos or Mexican Americans . . . This fallacy serves to create the new stereotype which is found in the completion of the statement, Mexican American children are . . .' (quoted in Gibson, 1984, p. 100).

The rather disturbing and contradictory findings of Baker (1973), Fish (1981) and Buckingham (1984), and the complaints about methods and content raised by minority educators such as Garcia (1974), have cast doubt on the educational and practical value of cultural understanding approaches to racial differences in schooling. Some proponents of multicultural education have therefore suggested different curriculum and instructional approaches to race relations in school. These curriculum theorists, led by educators such as Banks (1981, 1987), assert that all students should be able to demonstrate cultural competence in the language and cultural practices of ethnic groups other than their own.

Models of Cultural Competence

Underpinning the cultural competence approach to multicultural education is a fundamental assumption that values of cultural pluralism should have a central place in the school curriculum. This concept of social institutions as representing a plurality of ethnic interests was first formulated by liberal social scientists such as Riesman, Glazer and Denney (1969) and Glazer and Moynihan (1963). Some educators such as Banks (1981, 1987), Cortes (1973), Pettigrew (1974) and Gollnick (1980), contend that there is a general lack of cross-cultural competencies, especially in the area of language, among minority and majority groups in the American populace. These educators argue for various forms of bilingual, bicultural and ethnic studies programs based on pluralist values. These programs aim at preserving cultural diversity in the United States, particularly the language and identity of minority groups such as blacks, Hispanics and Native Americans. Banks (1981) summarizes this pluralist approach to ethnic differences in the following manner:

> The pluralist argues that ethnicity and ethnic identities are very important in American society. The United States, according to the pluralist, is made up of competing ethnic groups, each of which champions its economic and political interests. It is extremely important, argues the pluralist, for the individual to

develop a commitment to his or her ethnic group, especially if that ethnic group is 'oppressed' by more powerful ethnic groups within American society. (p. 62)

The American Association of Colleges for Teacher Education (AACTE) in their often-cited 'No One American Model', also make a paricularly strong case for cultural pluralism in education. AACTE maintains that:

Multicultural education is education which values cultural pluralism. Multicultural education rejects the view that schools should merely tolerate cultural pluralism. Instead, multicultural education affirms that schools should be oriented toward the cultural enrichment of all children and youth through programs rooted to the preservation and extension of cultural alternatives. Multicultural education recognizes cultural diversity as a fact of life in American society, and it affirms that this cultural diversity is a valuable resource that should be preserved and extended. It affirms that major education institutions should strive to preserve and enhance cultural pluralism. 1973, p. 264)

Proponents of multicultural education as cultural competence, such as the AACTE's Commission on Multicultural Education (1973), argue that multiculturalism in education should mean more than the fostering of cultural understanding and awareness about America's ethnic groups. They argue that 'teachers [should] help students develop ethnic identities, knowledge about different cultural groups ... and competence in more than one cultural system' (Grant and Sleeter, 1985, p. 101). By integrating the language and culture of a plurality of ethnic groups into the curriculum, proponents argue that teachers can help to 'build bridges' between America's different ethnic groups (Sleeter and Grant, 1986, p. 4). The target population of this cultural competence approach to multicultural education is mainly minority students. It is expected that minority students will develop competence in the 'public culture' and the skills and the attitudes of the dominant white society (Lewis, 1976, p. 35). But this familiarity with mainstream culture must not take place at the expense of the minority student's own ethnic heritage — a difficult balancing act indeed.

The cultural competence approach to multicultural education is underpinned by some basic assumptions about race relations in education and society in the United States. The following are some of the principal ideological assumptions and values of the cultural competence approach:

a) Previous assimilationist approaches to education, which characterized the United States as a melting pot of ethnic groups, actually helped to foster the hegemony of Anglo values. This has led to the virtual subordination or exclusion of minority culture from the American mainstream (Banks, 1981, 1987).

b) Cross-cultural interaction through bilingual/bicultural education programs will help to guarantee the survival of minority language and minority culture (Cortes, 1973; Ramirez and Castenada, 1974).

c) Cross-cultural interaction between America's ethnic groups is regarded as a powerful antidote to the racial prejudice that continues to limit the presence of blacks, Hispanics and Native Americans in America's mainstream (Grant and Sleeter, 1989).

Educational theorists who advocate the cultural competence approach to multicultural education champion a pluralism which has as its principal objective the preservation of minority language and culture. Bicultural and bilingual programs associated with this cultural competence approach aim to prepare minority students for their social and cultural negotiation with dominant white mainstream society. At the same time, it is expected that white students will also acquire knowledge and familiarity with the language and culture of minority groups. It is felt that such cross-cultural interaction will contribute to reduced antagonism between majority and minority ethnic groups.

Proponents of the cultural competence approach have attempted to develop programs that go beyond cultural awareness and attitudinal change. This approach to multiculturalism is particularly critical of earlier compensatory education programs, which worked centrally on the assumption that minority students were 'culturally deficient'. Instead, proponents of models of cross-cultural competence valorize minority cultural heritage and language and argue for the meaningful inclusion in the curriculum of 'aspects of minority culture that a teacher could build on' (Sleeter and Grant, 1986, p. 4).

But the emphasis on cultural competence as a set of curricular strategies for enhancing minority negotiation with mainstream society precipitates a central contradiction. On the one hand, the affirmation of minority culture in various bilingual, bicultural and ethnic studies programs represents a direct challenge to the centrality of Anglo values in the school curriculm and the notion that minority culture and language are 'naturally' deficient (Banks, 1987; McCarthy, 1988). On the other, the closely related objective of 'building bridges' (Sleeter and Grant, 1986, p. 4) from minority groups to mainstream society privileges individual mobility over a collective identity politics oriented toward change in the current structure of race relations in schools and society. In this way, the cultural competence approach has a significant unintended consequence. Attempts to teach minority students how to cross over to the language and culture of mainstream America also commit these students to a trajectory that leads toward incorporation and assimilation — an educational and social result that is antithetical to one of the principal concerns of the advocates of biculturalism — the valorization and preservation of minority cultural identities.

In sum, then, within the parlance of those who promote the cultural competence model, despite the emphasis on diversity, the minority child is just like anbody else's, free to make his or her choices in the marketplace of culture, ethnicity and heritage. As Banks (1987) argues, '[Minority and majority] students need to learn that there are cultural and ethnic alternatives within our society that they can freely embrace' (p. 12). Presumably, the responsibility that the enterprising minority youth undertakes in exchange for his participation in the cultural marketplace is that of respecting the society's institutions and the rules that make them 'work' for those in the American mainstream.

Within recent years, challenges to the cultural understanding and cultural competence approaches to muticulturalism have led to the reformulation and reconceptualization of multicultural perspectives on racial inequality in education. Proponents of multicultural education such as Suzuki (1979, 1984) and Swartz (1989) link the current demands for multiculturalism to a more reformist policy discourse of cultural emancipation and social reconstruction. It is this policy discourse that I would now like to discuss.

Models of Cultural Emancipation and Social Reconstruction

Like proponents of curriculum and educational policies of cultural understanding and cultural competence, educators who promote the idea of cultural emancipation within the framework of multicultural-ism attach a positive value to minority culture (Grant and Sleeter, 1989; Suzuki, 1984; Swartz, 1989). These educators argue that multiculturalism in education can promote the cultural emancipation and social amelioration of minority youth in two vital ways. First, proponents of emancipatory multiculturalism argue that the fostering of universal respect for the individual ethnic history, culture and language of the plurality of students to be found in American schools will have a positive effect on individual minority self-concepts. Positive self-concepts should in turn help to boost achievement among minority youth (Bullivant, 1981). This first set of claims therefore retraces some of the ground of the cultural deprivation theorists in that it is suggested that minority students do poorly in school because of their lack of self-esteem, among other things.

But proponents of emancipatory multiculturalism add a new twist. They link the issue of minority underachievement in the classroom to the attitudinal prejudice of teachers and the suppression of minority culture in the school curriculum. These reformist educators then argue that a reversal in teacher attitudes and in curriculum and instructional policies that suppress minority cultural identities would have a positive effect on minority school achievement. Individual minority school performance would improve since such students would be motivated by a multicultural curriculum and classroom environment in which teachers and students treat minority culture and experiences with respect (Olneck, 1989). For example, Swartz (1989) insists that students who come from family backgrounds in which ethnic pride and identity are emphasized are likely to do well in school, or at least better than those who do not:

> A curriculum which values diverse cultures in an equitable way is self-affirming ... It makes a statement to students about the importance of their present and future roles as participants and contributors to society. Research findings by Cummins (1984) and Ogbu (1978) point out that significant school failure does not occur in cultural groups that are positively oriented toward both their own and others' cultures. These students demonstrate a higher educational success rate. (p. 6)

The second conceptual strand of this emancipatory agenda is related to the first, but more directly links race relations in the classroom to the economy. Proponents of multicultural education as an emancipatory program suggest that improved academic achievement would help minority youth break the cycle of poverty and missed opportunity created by a previous biography of cultural deprivation.

The labor market is expected to verify emancipatory multicultural programs by absorbing large numbers of qualified minority youth. This thesis of a 'tightening bond' between multicultural education and the economy is summarized in the following claim by James Rushton (1981):

> The curriculum in the multicultural school should encourage each pupil to succeed wherever he or she can and strive for competence in what he or she tries. Cultural taboos should be lessened by mutual experience and understandings. The curriculum in the multicultural school should allow these things to happen. If it does, it need have no fear about the future career of its pupils. (p. 169)

This emancipatory or 'benevolent' type of approach to multicultural education (Gibson 1984; Troyna and Williams, 1986) rests, in part, on an earlier curriculum philosophy of 'social reconstructionism'. Like earlier curriculum theorists such as Rugg (1932) and Counts (1932), proponents of the emancipatory approach to multiculturalism offer the powerful ideology of the 'quiet revolution'. They suggest that cultural and social changes in minority fortunes are possible if the school curriculum is redefined in response to the needs of minority youth (Grant and Sleeter, 1989; Troyna and Williams, 1986).

Proponents of emancipatory multiculturalism operate on some basic assumptions about the role of education in the reproduction and transformation of race relations:

a)   There is a fundamental mismatch between the school curriculum and the life experiences and cultural backgrounds of American minority youth (Swartz, 1989).

b)   This mismatch exists because schools privilege white middle-class values while simultaneously suppressing the culture of minority youth (Williams, 1982).

c)   Thus, schools play a critical role in the production of differential educational opportunities and life chances for minority and majority youth.

d)   Educators should help to redress this pattern of inequality by embarking upon multicultural curricular reform that would provide equality of opportunity for academic success for minority students.

A genuine multicultural curriculum which includes knowledge about minority history and cultural achievements would reduce the dissonance and alienation from academic success that centrally characterizes minority experiences in schooling in the United States. Such a reformed school curriculum is expected to enhance minority opportunities for academic success and better futures in the labor market. And, in keeping with this thesis, employers are expected to allocate jobs on the basis of market-rational criteria, namely, the credentials and academic qualifications of prospective minority employees (Bullivant, 1981; Rushton, 1981).

Educators who subscribe to the emancipatory approach to multicultural education offer a 'language of possibility' (Giroux, 1985) with respect to the school curriculum — a language that is not present in earlier assimilationist frameworks. In an ideological sense, such a multicultural program allows for the possibility that the scope of current school knowledge will be 'enlarged' to include the radical diversity of knowledge(s), histories and experiences of marginalized ethnic groups. It is possible, for example, that radical ideas associated with minority quests for social change will also find their way into the discourse of the classrom (Olneck, 1983).

In addition, the powerfully attractive social reconstructionist theme running through the thesis of emancipatory multiculturalism raises the possibility of equality in the job market itself. Models of cultural understanding or cultural competence tend not to venture so far beyond the textbook, the classroom and the school.

However, radical school theorists have, with good reason, criticized the tendency of these multicultural proponents to lean toward an unwarranted optimism about the impact of the multicultural curriculum on the social and economic futures of minority students (McLaren and Dantley, in press; Mullard, 1985; Troyna and Williams, 1986). Indeed, the linear connection between academic credentials and the economy asserted by proponents of multicultural education is problematic. The assumption that higher educational attainment and achievement via a more sensitive curriculum would lead to a necessary conversion into jobs for black and minority youth is frustrated by the existence of racial practices in the job market itself. Troyna (1984) and Blackburn and Mann (1979), in their incisive analyses of the British job market, explode the myth that these is a necessary 'tightening bond' between education and the economy. In his investigation of the fortunes of 'educated' black and white youth in the job market, Troyna (1984) concludes that racial and social connections, rather than educational qualifications per se, 'determined' the phenomenon of better job chances for white youth even when black youth had higher qualifications than their white counterparts. The tendency of employers to rely on informal channels or word-of-mouth networks, and the greater likelihood that white youth would be in a position to exploit such networks, constitute one of the principal ways in which the potential for success of qualified black youth in the labor market is systematically undermined. Carmichael and Hamilton (1967) and Marable (1983) have made similar arguments about the racial disqualification of black youth in the job market in the United States. Expanding this argument, Crichlow (1985) makes the following claim:

> In combination with subtle forms of discrimination, job relocation, and increasing competition among workers for smaller mumbers of 'good' jobs, rising entry level job requirements clearly underscore the present employment difficulties experienced by young black workers. Whether they possess a high school diploma or not, blacks, in this instance, continue to experience high rates of unemployment despite possessing sound educational backgrounds and potential (capital) to be productive workers. (p. 6)

But there is more wrong with the multicultural thesis than naivete about the racial character of the job market. Proponents of multicultural education as an emancipatory formula tend to ignore the complex social and political relations that are constituted in the internal order of the schools. Issues of policy formation, decision-making, trade-offs and the building of alliances for specific reformist initiatives have not really been addressed within multicultural frameworks. For these reformist educators, educational change hinges almost exclusively upon the reorganization of the content of the school curriculum. But as Troyna and Williams (1986) have pointed out, attempts at the reorganization of the school curriculum to include more historically and culturally sensitive materials on minorities have not significantly affected the unequal relations that exist between blacks and whites in schools and in society.

School critics such as Mullard (1985) also contend that the underlying assumptions of multicultural education are fundamentally idealistic. As such, the structural and material relations in which racial antagonism is embedded are underemphasized. This has a costly result. By focusing on sensitivity training and on individual differences, multicultural proponents typically skirt the very problem which multicultural education seeks to address: WHITE RACISM. The progressive teachers' organization ALTARF (All London Teachers Against Racism and Fascism), in their volume *Challenging Racism* (1984), berate the multicultural program in London on precisely these grounds:

> These years have witnessed the growing acceptance by LEA [local educational authorities] of a bland and totally depoliticized form of multicultural education alongside the intensification of state racism in the form of ever increasing deportations, police brutality against Black people, discrimination in employment and harassment unemployment. (p. 1)

It is criticisms such as those advanced by ALTARF, Troyna and Williams, and Mullard that have seriously called into question the validity of liberal reformist claims about the emancipatory potential of multicultural education and its ability to positively influence minority futures in schools and society in the United States.

Conclusion

Spurred forward by minority group pressure for equality of opportunity in education and society, and by the efforts of liberal scholars to provide practical solutions to racial inequality, multicultural education became one of the most powerful educational slogans in the 1970s and 1980s. Federal legislation for ethnic studies and bilingual programs reinforced the state's ideological commitment to multicultural approaches to racial differences in schooling (Grant and Sleeter, 1989). A growing number of school districts and university-based teacher education preservice programs have also espoused various forms of multicultural education (Baker, 1977; Swartz, 1989). In this chapter, I have explored the conceptual and practical claims of three approaches to or discourses of multicultural education. I have described these approaches as models of cultural understanding, cultural competence and cultural emancipation. As we saw, each of these approaches represents a subtly different inflection on the question of what is to be done about racial inequality in schooling. Thus, proponents of cultural understanding advocate sensitivity and appreciation of cultural differences — a model for racial harmony. Cultural competence proponents insist on the preservation of minority ethnic identity and language and 'the building of bridges' between minority and mainstream culture. Finally, models of cultural emancipation go somewhat further than the previous two approaches in suggesting that a reformist multi-cultural curriculum can boost the school success and economic futures of minority youth.

But as I have tried to show, these multicultural approaches to curriculum reform really do not offer viable explanations of or 'solutions' to the problem of racial inequality in schooling. Within these frameworks, school reform and reform in race relations depend almost exclusively on the reversal of values, attitudes and the human nature of social actors understood as 'individuals'. Schools, for example, are not conceptualized as sites of power or contestation in which differential interests, resources and capacities determine the maneuverability of competing racial groups and the possibility and pace of change. In significant ways, too, proponents of multiculturalism fail to take into account the differential structure of opportunities that help to define minority relations to dominant white groups and social institutions in the United States. In abandoning the crucial issues of structural inequality and differential power relations, multicultural proponents end up placing an enormous responsibility on the shoulders of the classroom teacher in the struggle to transform race relations in American schools and society. These issues of structural analysis and political economy of race relations are more directly taken up by neo-Marxist school theorists, whose theories of racial inequality in schooling I will discuss in the next chapter.

Chapter 4

Neo-Marxist Approaches to Racial Inequality: The Subordination of the Problem of Race

As we saw in Chapters 2 and 3, mainstream liberal and multicultural educators treat 'culture' and 'values' as the principal explanatory variables in their analyses of racial inequality in schooling and in their prescriptions for educational reform. In sharp contrast, the neo-Marxist theorists and sociologists of education, whose work I will be discussing in this chapter, reject the starting points and conclusions generated within mainstream frameworks concerning the reproduction of racial inequality and educational differences (Henriques, 1984; Sarup, 1986). These radical theorists maintain that mainstream attempts to cast the problem of racial domination in schooling in terms of attitudes, values and psychological differences are grossly inadequate. They argue further that the liberal preoccupation with the domain of values and individual achievement serves to divert our attention from the integral relationship that exists between schools and a highly differentiated economy and power structure. These arguments have become more complicated over the past decade, but basically, radical writers have asserted that the problems of social difference and inequality are firmly rooted in the socioeconomic relations and structures generated within capitalist societies such as the United States. In so doing, they have sought to underscore the fact that, in their view, sites within the economy, not the school, are the critical arenas of capitalism and the 'fulcrums of change' (Carew, 1984).

   Not all radical educational theorists have taken this approach. Within the last fifteen years or so, growing dissatisfaction with Marxist dogmatism and economistic accounts of education have in part stimulated the rise of sustained cultural analyses of American schooling and society (Apple, 1982, 1986; Aronowitz and Giroux, 1985; Roman, Christian-Smith and Ellsworth, 1988; Wexler, 1982, 1987). Like mainstream theories, radical approaches to the issue of racial inequality in schooling are not monolithic. These different approaches within radical educational research have been described as 'structuralist' or 'culturalist' theories of education (Whitty, 1985; Weis, 1988). Though this classification does not quite capture the range of nuance that exists within current radical critiques of American schooling, it nevertheless draws attention to prevailing tensions within neo-Marxist research traditions. It would be useful at this stage to retrace some of the ground covered by neo-Marxist theorists over the last two decades or so.

Early Structuralist Theories of American Schooling and Society

Early radical critiques of schooling unproblematically narrowed the concerns over American education to the contradiction between capital and labor and the role of schooling in the maintenance and reproduction of the economy. These at least were the dominant themes to be found in the radical accounts of schooling written in the late 1960s and early 1970s. Carnoy's *Schooling in a Corporate Society* (1972), Spring's *Education and the Rise of the Corporate State* (1972) and Raskin's *Being and Doing* (1971) are particularly good examples of this economistic trend in radical critiques of schooling. These neo-Marxist theorists subscribed to orthodox analyses of capitalist society in the tradition of Baran (1957) and Baran and Sweezy (1966). Thus, these writers overwhelmingly emphasized the role of schooling in the maintenance and the reproduction of the capitalist division of labor. In this context, women and people of color were defined largely by their absence as independent forces.

It was perhaps Bowles and Gintis' *Schooling in Capitalist America* (1976) that represented the capstone of these structuralist and economistic accounts of education. Their analysis of American education was essentially functionalist. For these writers, schools existed in a closed relationship with the economy. Bowles and Gintis conceptualized the ideological and cultural features of the school as being responsible for a narrow range of determinations and effects — those stimulated by the economy. As they put it, 'Major aspects of educational organization replicate the relationship in the economic sphere' (p. 125). In Bowles and Gintis' account, schools functionally reproduced or mirrored the class structure and the segmented labor market. Racial inequality in schooling was conceptualized within these structuralist formulations as an effect of economic divisions in society and as a by-product of a more fundamental conflict between the working class and their capitalist employers. The specific content of racial oppression was seen as consisting of divisive ideologies orchestrated and deployed by capitalists and their agents in the labor market and the firm (Roemer, 1979). The particular effect of such capitalist strategies, it was claimed, was that of disorganizing the working class. A variant of this 'divide and conquer' explanation of racial and sexual antagonism has been offered recently by Edari (1984), who asserts that:

> Ethnicity, racism, and sexism must be understood in the proper perspective as forms of ideological mystification designed to facilitate exploitation and weaken the collective power of the laboring class. (p. 8)

In many ways, then, early structuralist accounts of schooling and society theorized racial phenomena in consistently negative terms, as forms of pre-capitalist particularism that served to divert or interrupt the major drama between the bourgeoisie and the working class (James, 1980). Thus racial domination has been located in the following historical and contemporary dynamics:

(a) *super-exploitation*, with racial coercion and exploitation in slavery as one of the earliest sources of surplus value (Blauner, 1972; Hechter, 1975);

(b) capitalist strategies of *divide and conquer* of an essentially passive working class, in which, as for example Jackubowicz (1985) argues, 'ethnicity has become a major locus of class struggle, an avenue used by dominant forces ... to fragment the working class' (p. 61); and

(c) a *split or discontinuous labor market*, in which the entrance of minorities and women depresses the wage scale and undermines existing privileges that a predominantly white male labor aristocracy enjoys (Bonacich, 1980, 1981; Reich, 1981).

Schooling is only a reflection of these structures. Bowles and Gintis (1976), for instance, maintained that the educational system prepares minority and working-class youth for the lower rungs of occupations in a hierarchically arranged job market. This is achieved,

they argued, by means of a 'correspondence' between the social relations of school and the social relations of capitalist production. What
really matters in an understanding of the process of subordination of
working-class and minority students is not 'school knowledge' per se,
but what Bowles and Gintis called the 'hidden curriculum'. By hidden
curriculum, Bowles and Gintis were referring to the largely unnoticed
structural relations of domination and subordination that are reproduced in teachers' pedagogical practices and exchanges with minority
and working-class youth. According to these authors, the hidden
curriculum is the mechanism that serves to reproduce the specific
norms, values and personality types needed in the secondary labor
market.

In a general sense, then, early structuralist accounts of racial inequality marginalized schooling and privileged both the economy and
class relations. Insofar as racially based antagonisms existed in schooling, they were construed as the results of causes located exogenously
in the paid workplace and in economic production. Although they
offered a clearer picture than most mainstream theorists of how inequality was produced, by basing their entire evaluation of schooling
on a base-superstructure model of society in which all significant
activity flowed from the base, these writers lost sight of the specific
and autonomous contribution of schooling to the nature of social life
and social relations in general. Because of this, they were unable to
deal adequately with the question of the relatively autonomous workings of patriarchal and racial structures that exist in American education and society. In the process, they also had the negative effect of
ignoring what some liberal researchers had contributed: a greater
sense of the importance of looking inside the schools to examine what
educational institutions really do culturally, politically and economically.

Radical Theories of Cultural Reproduction

American radical educators took a decisively more culturalist
approach to schooling in the mid-1970s partly out of a dissatisfaction
with structural economic explanations of schooling and society. These
critics complained of the tendency of orthodox Marxist educational
critics to: (a) reduce all the activities of school and society to the
singular operations and requirements of the economy; (b) define class
in narrow and restrictive economic terms; and (c) marginalize the
significance and effects of the school curriculum (Apple, 1979;

Giroux, 1985; Wexler, 1982). They insisted that structural economic accounts of education ignored the internal order, autonomous organization and social relations which specifically characterized schooling. These school critics, such as Apple (1979), Anyon (1979) and Giroux (1981, 1983), described themselves as theorists of cultural reproduction. Their writings absorbed and distilled a wide array of intellectual influences from continental Europe. These influences on American cultural reproduction theorists included the cultural Marxism of E.P. Thompson, Raymond Williams, Basil Bernstein and Pierre Bordieu, the critical theories of the Frankfurt School (Adorno, Horkeimer, *et al.*), and the work of Jürgen Habermas. A much more important influence, though, was exerted by the primarily British-generated 'new' sociology of education (particularly the work of Young, Esland, *et al.*, and their volume *Knowledge and Control*, 1971). But despite these European influences, most of the direct impulse for cultural reproduction theory came from within the United States itself in the form of the phenomenological critiques of schooling, such as those of Huebner (1968), Greene (1971) and MacDonald and Leeper (1966).

Both the new sociology of education theorists and American phenomenologists sought to render existing liberal accounts of school knowledge problematic. For instance, they directed attention to the human interests implicated in mainstream research and to the processes of organization and selection that informed the definition of what was taken for granted as school knowledge. (They sought to relate 'the principles of selection and organization that underlie curricula to their institutional and interactional setting in schools and classrooms and to the wider social structure', Young, quoted in Whitty, 1985, p. 7.) However, the overwhelming sense of humanist individualism embodied in these formulations was expressed in the somewhat naive belief that the re-orientation of school knowledge and pedagogical practices could achieve fundamental changes in the social and structural organization of school and society. Cultural reproduction theorists rejected the restrictive and 'idealist' phenomenological prescriptions of the new sociology of education and opted for a neo–Marxist approach which sought to establish links between school knowledge and issues of social inequality and political economy. At the same time, these American cultural critics sought to distance themselves from the economic reductionism of earlier structuralist formulations that had so clearly subordinated school life to the economy.

Writers such as Anyon (1979), Giroux (1981) and Wexler (1982) insisted that the ideological and cultural processes of schooling were relatively autonomous from the society's economic infrastructures.

Expanding on the arguments of continental educators such as Bordieu and Passeron (1977), cultural reproduction theorists maintained that the inner workings of school knowledge contributed a systematic advantage to white middle-class youth. Anyon (1979) argued that schools legitimated the dominant Anglo-American culture. The critical question to be asked about the school curriculum, one of these radical educators argued, was 'Whose knowledge was in the school and whose interests did such knowledge serve?' (Apple, 1979, p. 7). This ideological analysis of the strategic implications of school knowledge, its silences and its deletions of the self-affirming history of the oppressed was of fundamental demystificatory importance. The explicit attempt to link knowledge to power also partially opened up a fecund ground of possibilities for the investigation and exploration of school life around issues of the formation and constitution of racial and gender identities and representations. Unfortunately, however, these 'non-economic' themes were theoretically underdeveloped in cultural reproduction theory and were regrettably not followed through by radical researchers at the time. Instead, in their early work, cultural reproduction theorists chose to follow the well-tried and less knotty path of reading off ideological and cultural homologies between the formal school curriculum and class divisions outside the school. Nevertheless, there were some important gains made with respect to the examination of the issue of inequality in school and society. As Apple (1982), Bernstein (1982) and others had documented, a bipolar theory of class was insufficient in understanding schooling. The roles of the 'new middle class' and of conflict within classes became much clearer. Furthermore, the ability to specify what was actually happening to the work of teachers as their own labor was being transformed and 'deskilled', and how these teachers were responding to these pressures, was a significant advance over structural theories that saw teachers as merely puppets (Apple, 1986). But even with these gains, these more culturalist researchers usually retained a research practice of venerating class-motivated questions in the evaluation of the school curriculum. And all too often as well, they employed a determinist version of class. In this respect, a rigorous examination of the non-class and specifically racial features of American school life was deferred.

In the past few years, a new school of radical education theorists has begun to take up the challenge of formulating a more highly textured and nuanced account of schooling that has allowed for a more systematic exploration of the non-economic, non-class features of school life without at the same time ignoring economic and class dynamics. It is to this work and its implications for the conceptualization of racial inequality that I now wish to turn.

Critical Curriculum Theorists

In the late 1970s and early 1980s, challenges to some of the still reductive neo-Marxist interpretations of schooling and society came from two broad sources: one, theory, the other, political life. With respect to theory, feminist and race relations theorists in Europe and the United States (McRobbie, 1978; O'Brien, 1984; Omi and Winant, 1981, 1983; Sarup, 1986) and post-structuralist writers in the fields of linguistics, literary theory and psychoanalysis (Eagleton, 1983; Hicks, 1981; Irigaray, 1985; Kuhn, 1982) drew attention to the inadequacy of class-reductionist accounts of human society, the marginalization of women and minorities in radical research and to the underdeveloped status of radical conceptualizations of human agency, human subjectivity and systems of meaning.

In the area of politics, there were significant new developments, as reflected in the emergence of a plurality of social movements among subordinated groups. As women, gays, minorities and others mobilized around distinctly non-class agendas, neo-conservative groups soon offered a countervailing agenda expressed in terms of a highly vocal authoritarian populism (Apple, 1988). Orthodox class categories simply could not cope with these non-class movements or with the right-wing populist backlash in the government and the larger society (Aronowitz and Giroux, 1985; Omi and Winant, 1986). Somehow, radical theorists of the late 1970s and early 1980s seemed overtaken by the rising tide of consciousness among the new political movements (Popkewitz, 1987; Whitty, 1985).

These developments had sobering effects on radical school critics and engendered reappraisals, self-criticism and the emergence of yet another inflection on previous radical accounts of schooling in the form of critical curriculum theory. The work of critical curriculum theorists and sociologists of education such as Dale (1982), Hogan (1982), Popkewitz (1984, 1987), Wexler (1982, 1987) and the later writings of Apple (1982, 1986, 1988) departed in two important ways from that of earlier proponents of economic or cultural reproduction. First, though the metaphor of 'reproduction' was regarded as highly pertinent to an exploration of the relationship between schooling and capitalism, critical theorists argued that previous models of 'reproduction as reflection' were inadequate because they subordinated the agency of school actors. Critical theorists maintained that the school played a more active 'mediational' role in its relationship to a highly differentiated economy and society. Second, these school theorists offered significantly new understandings of the state's relationship to education and to social and economic inequality (Carnoy, 1984). Earlier formulations had, for example, assumed that all aspects of governmental functions (including education) reproduced what was economically 'necessary'. But the emerging critical literature on the state indicated a much more complicated process in which the state has its own needs — needs that are sometimes incongruent with the interests of capital and dominant classes. This focus on government and on the political sphere helped to expand the widening critique of economic and class reductionism as well (Dale, 1982).

Relative Autonomy, Mediation and Cultural Resistance

Perhaps it was Wexler (1982), in his germinal piece, 'Structure, Text, and Subject: A Critical Sociology of School Knowledge', who most poignantly announced the growing dissatisfaction with what he called 'reproduction' and 'reflection' models of schooling and society. Wexler maintained that in the discourse of cultural and economic reproduction, 'conscious rational human activity is dissolved between the poles of manipulative human ralations and iron-like system laws' (p. 276). He emphasized further that 'the system's reproductive perspective leads to forgetting that social structures are the result of human activity' (p. 276). School critics such as Wexler sought to emphasize even more strongly the relative autonomy of education and the contested nature of the internal social relations in the school itself. Of great importance, too, was the notion, advanced by Wexler and others, that social inequality was not only 'structural', but was embodied in the lived experiences and 'cultures' of social actors. 'Inequality', these writers argued, was produced as a consequence of political struggles and competing political projects among contending social groups.

Many of these new directions were indicated in a collected volume, *Ideology and Practice in Schooling* (Apple and Weis, 1983), which embarked on an ambitious theoretical and empirical project of critically evaluating both the 'commodified' and the 'lived' culture of school. These authors attempted to shed light on racial and sexual ideological practices in schooling. They offered an interactive view of the social formation that went beyond a focus only on class and emphasized the interrelations among racial, classed and gendered dynamics (a matter that will be addressed more fully in Chapter 5).

Writers in this volume, such as Anyon, Apple and Taxel, took the debate over the reproduction of inequality in the commodified school curriculum one step further than had previous radical researchers. These critical curriculum theorists set out to show that ideological and cultural differentiation is achieved not merely in the messages and themes 'encoded' in the content of school materials, but also in the manipulation of the form and organization of the school curriculum. Thus, for example, the author of the essay 'Curricular Form and the Logic of Technical Control' (Apple, 1983) sought to show that while the content of packaged curricula forged an ideological message that valorized the 'possessive individual', the standardized methods of presentation and routinized organization of this content 'constrained teachers in ways that made it difficult to organize the social relations of the classroom in a manner that would contest the messages implicit in the materials' (Whitty, 1985, p. 48). In a related sense, Anyon (1983), in her study of the treatment of labor and economic history in social studies texts, and Taxel (1983), in his analysis of the ideological reconstruction of the American revolution in children's fiction, drew attention to the systematic absence or exclusion of the point of view of subordinated groups. These writers suggested that this process of 'non-selection' had the effect of 'consolidating' the marginalization of working–class and minority identities in the social studies curriculum.

Critical curriculum theorists complemented their analyses of commodified school culture with a number of methodologically sophisticated and highly textured ethnographies of classroom life and the subcultures of resistance among principally working-class boys and girls. The work of Everhart (1983), Valli (1983), McNeil (1983) and Weis (1983) demonstrated that the schools were sites for identity formation. These student subcultures involved elements of both consent and resistance to the dominant school order. For example, Valli, in her study of the subculture of 'femininity' among young women enrolled in a high school secretarial education program, showed that the institutional culture generated among these students influenced the reproduction of their consent to second–class secretarial and clerical jobs. But Valli also drew attention to cultural contradictions between the feminine identities cultivated in the girls' business education program and capitalist economic needs for worker 'productivity'. Thus she concluded that the preparation for 'office work as either secondary to or synonymous with a sexual/house/family identity . . . marginalized these students' work identities. The culture of femininity associated with office work made it easier for them to be *less* attached to their work and their workplace than men, who stay in paid employment because they must live up to a masculine ideology of male-as-provider' (Valli, 1983, p. 232).

More recent writings by Popkewitz (1987), Roman, Christian-Smith and Ellsworth (1988), and Wexler (1987) have sought to extend critical analyses of the institutional culture of schools even further. These writers employ 'new' methodological strategies of semiotics, discourse analysis and materialist ethnography in their analyses of the construction and representation of teachers and students in the formal and informal life of the school and the community. In the writings of these critical theorists, our understanding of the role that language and representation in textbooks, in the classroom and in popular culture play in the subordination of working-class women and men and minority youth has been expanded considerably.

The Hegemonic State

Besides these cogent examples of qualitative research undertaken by Anyon (1983), Taxel (1983) and Valli (1983), and the more recent work of Roman, Christian-Smith and Ellsworth (1988), critical curriculum theorists made several important conceptual advances in attempting to specify the nature of the linkages among schools, the state and unequal social relations within the American capitalist formation. Writers such as Dale (1982), Carnoy (1982, 1984) and Carnoy and Levin (1985) made the case for what Giroux (1983) called the 'hegemonic state'. Critical theories regarding the state rested on the following claims. First, it was argued that the state is not an 'instrument' (in the Milibandian sense) of a dominant class or class fraction. Instead, theorists now maintained that the state was itself a site of ongoing conflict among a 'plurality' of contending social groups (Apple, 1988; Dale, 1982). Second, these theorists insisted that the state should no longer be conceptualized simplistically as a functional reflex of the economic base. Theorists now conceptualized the state as an 'organization' (Omi and Winant, 1986) that actively served to define capitalist social and economic relations, often with consequences that were inconsistent with capitalism's 'needs'.

Drawing on the work of Offe, Ronge, Poulantzas and Gramsci, critical theorists of education conceptualized the state in terms of a network of social relations (national, regional, local, municipal and so forth) around which the organization of consent is secured. Here, the concept of 'hegemony' was pivotal to a re-examination of power in education and society. Power relations were now theorized less in terms of simple models of asymmetry in which the state enforces the 'will' of capital. Instead, it was argued that contradiction, variability and autonomy are constitutive and systematic features of the state's relationship to the economy. This new approach focused attention on the forging of alliances within the state. It was now recognized that the state is affected by myriad 'interventions' not only by capital, but by oppressed groups as well.

Conflicting demands on the state from contending social groups generates tension, fragmentation and crisis. The state, it was argued, consistently has to juggle the demands of accumulation with demands for social and political amelioration (social mobility and democratic participation) articulated by oppressed sectors of society. The hegemonic character of the state is expressed in the mediation and the processual prioritization of competing demands from contending social groups. Consequently, radical, emancipatory and even ameliorative agendas are systematically reinterpreted, redirected and often delegitimized and derailed.

It was also claimed that schools, as ideological apparatuses connected to the state, are deeply implicated in relations of domination and exploitation. Critical curriculum theorists explored the relationship between the state and schooling by investigating (a) the extent and the specific dimensions of the state's exercise of control over schooling in terms of the state's economic, political and ideological agenda (Carnoy and Levin, 1985; Dale, 1982); and (b) the processes by which the school not only mediates but obstructs the agenda of the state and the demands of capital (Apple, 1982, 1988). Carnoy and Levin (1985) maintained that the school has its own rationality. This exists, for example, in the form of liberal democratic values and a commonsense discourse of ethics and 'fair play' which thrives in schooling but which at the same time operates as a countervailing moment with respect to the instrumentalist demands of the economy. But, as Piven and Cloward (1979) have argued, neo-conservative educators have often sought to mobilize and rearticulate this educational discourse of 'fairness' as part of a strategy directed at subverting minority oppositional challenges to educational inequality. Legitimate challenges to racial inequality are countered by pointing to apparently neutral criteria of 'achievement', 'ability' and 'competence'. In this discourse of achievement, structural impediments to the forward motion of the oppressed are obscured and the criterion of 'individual merit' is elevated as the guiding principle of educational and social selection for rewards and commendation.

These developments in the theorization of the state and the relationship of the school curriculum to the production of inequality allowed critical theorists to make significant advances over earlier economic and cultural reproduction theories. Critical theorists now argued for greater flexibility in the examination of the relationship of schooling to ideology, culture, politics and the economy. These theorists also offered a more complex notion of state power which drew on the Gramscian concept of hegemony (the idea that power is mobilized through the organization of consent). These new insights helped to shift the discourse of Marxist and radical sociology of curriculum away from static issues of class composition and reproduction to an exploration of the transformative elements within the informal order of educational institutions and within the subcultural practices of working-class and minority youth.

Conclusion

In this chapter, I have tried to show the considerable variation that exists in radical theories of racial inequality in education. The principal contradictions within radical accounts of racial differences reside within (a) radical methods of appropriating racial antagonism in their formulations, and (b) the theoretical status accorded to race with respect to class in radical models of analysis of schooling and society. These contradictions are illustrated in the typology presented in Figure 4.1. This typology summarizes the differences among these approaches to schooling along the following dimensions: Dimension I ('level of abstraction') captures the level of abstraction at which class and racial inequality are theorized (social system on the one hand versus conjuncture or social institutional context on the other). Dimension II ('asymmetrical' versus 'symmetrical') summarizes the contradiction between asymmetry and symmetry in radical models of analysis of the relative 'weight' of the effects of class versus race on the school curriculum. Cells 1–4 identify different combinations of these dimensions as reflected in curriculum writings of radical educators.

The work of early structural economic sociologists of education

Figure 4.1 *Typology of radical curriculum accounts of race*

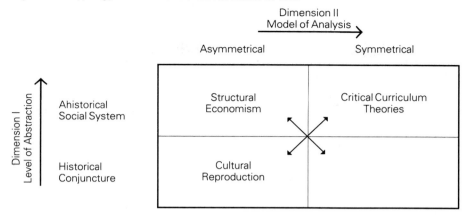

such as Bowles and Gintis (1976), for example, evaluates the relationship of race to schooling from the level of abstraction of the social system (a very abstract level indeed!). Race is subordinated to class in terms of the structural economic specification of what counts in the shaping of school life and societal effects beyond the school. Early structural economic theorists are therefore assigned to Cell 1. Like the early structuralists, critical curriculum theorists such as Apple (1988), Apple and Weis (1983) and Wexler (1982, 1987) also evaluate the relationship of race to schooling at the level of abstraction of the social system. But significantly, these writers offer an interactional or symmetrical model of social relations that attempts to avoid the privileging of class. Class, race and gender are theorized as having codeterminate effects on school life (Cell 3). Neo-Marxist theories of cultural reproduction, such as the early work of Apple (1979), Bernstein (1977) and Bordieu and Passeron (1977), are represented in Cell 2. Theorists of cultural reproduction emphasize the study of class relations at the conjunctural level in terms of the internal workings of schools. As I argued earlier, cultural reproduction theorists privileged class and deferred the question of racial inequality in their examination of the internal working of schools.

Despite this rich variety and the increasing subtlety of radical theories of curriculum and education, systematic theorization of racial dynamics at the conjunctural level of institutions such as schools remains underdeveloped within the neo-Marxist framework (hence the empty box, Cell 4). What, then, is the specificity of race? Under what conditions is a racial context likely to exist in schools? How should we understand its relationship to other dynamics? In the next chapter, I will offer an alternative approach to the problem of racial inequality that attempts to get at the dynamics of race relations as they operate at the institutional level of schooling.

Chapter 5

Nonsynchrony and Social Difference: An Alternative to Current Radical Accounts of Race and Schooling

Despite its limitations, the mainstream and radical educational literature on race relations in schooling has pointed us in some very important directions. For instance, we now know where some of the most significant tensions, stresses and gaps in our current research on social difference and inequality are. I believe that it is precisely these 'gaps', 'stresses', 'tensions' and discontinuities that must be explored if researchers are to begin to develop a more adequate account of the operation of racial inequality in education and society.

In the first part of this chapter, I will examine three areas which I consider crucial points of difference and tension between and within mainstream and radical approaches to racial inequality in the curriculum and educational literature. These areas can be summarized as follows: (a) the structure-culture distinction, (b) macro- versus micro-theoretical and methodological perspectives on race, and (c) the issue of historical variability versus essentialism in the designation of racial categories.

In the second part of this chapter, I will make the case for an alternative approach to racial inequality, which I shall call a *nonsynchronous theory* of race relations in schooling and society. In advancing the position of nonsynchrony, I will argue against 'essentialist' or single-cause explanations of the persistence of racial inequality in education that are currently being offered in both the mainstream and radical curriculum and educational literature. Instead, I will direct attention to the complex and contradictory nature of race relations in the institutional life of social organizations such as schools.

Let us first look at the principal tensions within mainstream and radical accounts of racial inequality.

Areas of Tension in Mainstream and Radical Research

Structure versus Culture

As I showed in Chapter 2, liberal educational theorists place a great deal of emphasis on 'values' as the site of the social motivation for the maintenance and persistence of racial inequality. This emphasis on values as a central explanatory variable in liberal theories of racial inequality should not be dismissed out of hand. The primary theoretical and practical merit of this liberal position resides in the fact that it seeks to restore human agency to the project of evaluating the relationship between social difference and education. Thus, for liberal theorists in their examination of racial antagonism in schooling, it is the active agency and subjectivities of students and teachers that really matter and that can make a difference in race relations.

In a related sense, liberal researchers also recognize the cultural role of education in initiating the social neophyte into dominant values, traditions and rituals of 'stratification' (Durkheim, 1977; Ogbu and Matute-Bianchi, 1986). But liberal pluralist researchers conceptualize racial values as emanating from a coherent Cartesian individual subject. When groups or social collectivities are invoked in liberal frameworks on racial inequality, they are specified in terms of aggregates of individuals. The problem here, as I indicated earlier, is that such an emphasis on individual agency also results in the undertheorization of the effectivity of social and economic structures in the determination of racial inequality.

This tension between structure and agency is also powerfully expressed within radical discourses. Neo-Marxists insist that racial domination must, in part, be understood in the context of capitalism's elaboration of macrostructures and not simply in terms of individual preferences. They draw our attention to the fact that racial domination is deeply implicated in the fundamental organization of specific human societies as well as in the evolution of capitalism as a world system. In this way, we come to understand race as a profoundly social category. Racial domination is thus conceptualized at the level of social collectivities and their differential and conflictual relationships to the means of production. This alerts us to the powerful connections among racial domination and economic inequality, differential material resources and capacities, and unequal access to social and political institutions such as schools.

But recent Marxist cultural criticism has sought to raise other issues concerning social difference and inequality in American education (Crichlow, 1990; Omi and Winant, 1986; Sarup, 1986). These issues — of identity, subjectivity, culture, language and agency — direct attention to the informal curriculum of schools and the sub-cultural practices of school youth. This theoretical development has taken place partly in response to the early work of radical school critics, such as Bowles and Gintis (1976), who tended to subordinate agency, meaning and subjectivity to economic structures (for example, the workplace) exogenous to the school. Writers such as Apple and Weis (1983) contend that previous neo–Marxist emphasis on economic structures focuses attention on only part of the puzzle in our investigation of racial inequality. In a similar manner, liberal emphasis on social and cultural 'values' as the primary site of racial antagonism provides us with only a partial understanding of the way in which racial dynamics operate. Marxist cultural theorists have therefore attempted to transcend the binary opposition of structure versus culture entailed in previous neo–Marxist and liberal theories by offering a more interactive view of the central contradictions in capitalist society. However, to the extent that some critical educational theorists have attempted to incorporate these more interactive perspectives into their examination of the relationship between schooling and inequality, these efforts have been directed almost exclusively toward understanding the dynamics of class, not race.

Macro- versus Microperspectives

There is a further bifurcation in the curriculum and educational literature on race: mainstream theorists have tended to focus more directly on microlevel classroom variables, while radical theorists have offered macroperspectives on racial inequality that have privileged areas outside the school, such as the economy and the labor process. As I indicated earlier, radical school critics have generally specified structural relations at such a high level of abstraction (the level of abstraction of the mode of production) that all human agency evaporates from their analysis of society. This abstract approach is also residually present in more recent critical curriculum studies of social difference and inequality in the institutional settings of schools (Apple, 1988; Giroux, 1985; Hogan, 1982; Whitty, 1985). As we saw in the previous chapter, these more culturalist theorists have argued that race is linked to other social dynamics, such as class and gender, in a system of multiple determinations. Sarup (1986) has quite persuasively argued that these 'additive' models of inequality have simply failed to capture the degree of nuance, variability, discontinuity and multiplicity of histories and 'realities' that exist in the school setting. In a similar manner, both Omi and Winant (1986) and Burawoy (1981) have pointed to the fact that the intersection of race and class can lead, for example, to the augmentation or diminution of racial solidarity, depending on the contingencies and variables in the local setting such as the school. All of this points toward the need for theoretical and practical work articulated at what Hall (1986) calls the 'middle range'. That is to say that it is important that radical theorists begin to specify more directly the ways in which race operates in the local context of schools.

Let me be clear about what is at issue here. I believe that the radical intuition that racial inequality is implicated and must be understood in the context of the development of capitalism's macrostructures is basically correct if it takes seriously the relatively autonomous workings of the state. On the other hand, unqualified liberal emphasis on individual motivation and rational action as the terms of reference for 'normal' behavior locates racism in idiosyncratic, arbitrary and abnormal attitudes and actions. This requires us to abandon materialist explanations of racial antagonism and seek recourse in differential psychology and so on. The burden and responsibility for the oppression of racial minorities are squarely placed on the shoulders of these irrational or 'authoritarian personalities' (Henriques, 1984). Even more problematic is the fact that change and transformation of these oppressive relations are made conditional upon the institutional reformation of these individuals and their return to the observance of rational norms that guide the society and its institutions. Needless to say, historical evidence and the very persistence of racial inequality in schools and society go against the grain of this thesis and the programmatic responses it has precipitated.

The Issue of History

Though both the macrological and micrological perspectives that underpin radical and liberal formulations give us a general map of racial logics, they do not tell us how movement is orchestrated, or realized along the grid of race relations. That is to say that neither current liberal nor neo-Marxist theories of schooling inform us about the historical trajectory of racial discourse and the struggles over such racial discourse within specific institutions such as education. There is indeed a tendency within mainstream and radical frameworks to treat racial definitions ('black', 'white', etc.) as immutable, *a priori* categories. Racial categories such as black and white are taken for granted within the popular common sense as well as in the writings of scholars in education. Associated with this tendency are tacit or explicit propositions about the origins of races and racism. Mainstream theorists identify the origin of the races in physical and psychological traits, geography, climate, patterns of ancient migrations and so on (Gould, 1981; Harris, 1968). Radical theorists, on the other hand, link race and racism to the specific event of the emergence of capitalism and its 'need' to rationalize the super-exploitation of African slave labor and the segmented division of labor (Bonacich, 1981; Williams, 1964). The major methodological problem of all of these 'origins' arguments is that they presume the eternal existence of racial distinctions and incorporate them into the analysis of racial antagonism as though such distinctions were functional social categories that have remained stable throughout history. In both mainstream and radical writings, then, 'race' is historically given. (After all, says our common sense, 'we know who black people and white people are merely by observation and inspection'.) The historical variability associated with racial categories and the social purposes that racial distinctions serve are consequently undertheorized.

But as Omi and Winant (1986) have argued, race is preeminently a 'social historical concept'. For example, it is only through developed social practices and the particular elaboration of historical and material relations in the US that 'white consciousness', with its associated category 'white people', emerged. Likewise, it is only through similar historical and social practices that racial 'others' — who in reality have varying economic and social positions — emerged under the definition of 'black', 'Asian', etc. In this sense, racial categories and 'the meaning of race and the definitions of specific racial groups have varied significantly over time and between different societies' (Omi and Winant, 1986, p. 61). A few examples are useful in helping to illustrate the instability and variability of racial categories.

In the United States, the racial classification 'white' evolved with the consolidation of slavery in the seventeenth century. Euro-American settlers of various 'ancestry' (Dutch, English and so forth) claimed a common identity in relation to exploited and enslaved African peoples. As Winthrop Jordan (1968) observes:

From the first, then, vis-a-vis 'Negro' the concept embedded in the term *Christian* seems to have conveyed much of the idea and feeling of 'we' against 'they': to be *Christian* was to be civilized rather than barbarous, English rather than African, white rather than black. The term *Christian* itself proved to have remarkable elasticity, for by the end of the seventeenth century it was being used to define a species of slavery which had altogether lost any connection with explicit religious difference. In the Virginia code of 1705, for example, the term sounded much more like a definition of race than of religion: 'And for a further christian care and usage of all christian servants, Be it also enacted, *by the authority aforesaid, and it is hereby enacted,* That no negroes, mulattos, or Indians, although christians, or Jews, Moors, Mahometans, or other infidels, shall, at any time, purchase any christian servant, nor any other, except of their own complexion, or such as are declared slaves by this act.' By this time 'Christianity' had somehow become intimately linked with 'complexion' . . . Most suggestive of all, there seems to have been something of a shift during the seventeenth century in the terminology which Englishmen in the colonies applied to themselves. From the initially most common term *Christian*, at mid-century there was a marked shift toward 'English' and 'free.' After about 1680, taking the colonies as a whole, a new term appeared — 'white.' (pp. 94–5)

It is through these same practices of inclusion and exclusion that the 'others' of colonial America — the enslaved African peoples — were defined as 'negro' or 'black'. Thus, the racial category 'negro' redefined and homogenized the plural identities of disparate African people whose 'ethnic origins' were Ibo, Yoruba, Fulani and so on.

Racial categories also vary contemporaneously between societies. For example, while the racial designation 'black' in the United States refers only to people of African descent, in England, oppressed Asian and Afro-Caribbean minorities have appropriated 'black' as a counter-hegemonic identity. In Latin America, racial categories are used and appropriated with a higher degree of flexibility than in the United States. Omi and Winant (1986), drawing on the work of cultural anthropologist Marvin Harris, foreground this variability and discontinuity in race relations in Latin America:

By contrast [to the United States], a striking feature of race relations in the lowland areas of Latin America since the abolition of slavery has been the relative absence of sharply defined racial groupings. No such rigid descent rule characterizes racial identity in many Latin American societies. Brazil, for example, has historically had less rigid conceptions of race, and thus a variety of 'intermediate' racial categories exist. Indeed, as Harris notes, 'One of the most striking consequences of the Brazilian system of racial identification is that parents and children and even brothers and sisters are frequently accepted as representatives of quite opposite racial types.' Such a possibility is incomprehensible within the logic of racial categories in the US. (p. 61)

Social practices of racial classification are elaborated and contested throughout society and within given institutions by personal and collective action. In this way racial definitions are reproduced and transformed. Historically, education has been a principal site for the reproduction and elaboration of racial meaning and racial identities. An examination of the career of racial discourses within the overall trajectory of curriculum and educational theories and practices rapidly disabuses us of the notion that education is a 'neutral' or 'innocent' institution with respect to racial struggles (JanMohamed, 1987; JanMohamed and Lloyd, 1987). An investigation of the genealogy of racial discourses in education would, for example, take us through the domains of:

1 Colonial/plantation America's education laws that prohibited the education of black Americans, such as the eighteenth-century statutes of South Carolina and other states (Jan-Mohamed and Lloyd, 1987, p. 7).
2 Jim Crow's educational policies in the North and the South that segregated and concentrated blacks and other minorities into inferior schools (Carnoy, 1974; Ogbu, 1978).
3 Mental measurement and human intelligence theories — from the laboratory of cranium estimates to the anthropological and biological theories of racial difference in the work of the likes of Morton (1839) and Gobineau (1915), and the genetics-based theories of race and intelligence of Eysenck and Kamin (1981) and Jensen (1969, 1981, 1984).
4 Curriculum theories of social efficiency, differential psychology and cultural deprivation that labeled black youth as 'under-

achievers', and have labeled black families and black communities as 'defective' and 'dysfunctional'.

5   Liberal and progressive-inspired educational programs such as Head Start, compensatory education and multicultural programs that have been aimed at helping to close the educational and cultural gap between black and white youth.

At every historical juncture of the racialization of dominant educational institutions in the United States, African Americans and other racial minorities have contested and have sought to redefine hegemonic conceptions of racial differences in 'intelligence' and 'achievement' and the curriculum strategies of inclusion and exclusion and selection that these commonsense racial theories have undergirded. Over the years, this cultural resistance has been mobilized on two principal fronts. On the one hand, since the period of Reconstruction, African Americans have conducted a 'war of maneuver' (Gramsci, 1983) outside the 'trenches' of dominant universities, schools and other educational centers by establishing parallel and alternative institutions of learning. While it is true that these institutions have not always been directed towards transformative projects, black educational institutions have provided a material basis for the nurturing of black intellectual and cultural autonomy (Marable, 1985; West, 1988).

Simultaneous with the elaboration of alternative institutions, African Americans and other minorities have conducted a 'war of position' (Gramsci, 1983) in the courts and the schools for equality of access to education. These struggles have also been enlarged to include insurgent challenges over a redefinition of dominant university academic programs. These challenges have directly influenced the emergence of the 'new' disciplines of ethnic studies, women's studies and so on, that have helped to broaden the range of knowledge and interests in the university setting.

Education has therefore played a central role in the drama of struggles over racial identities and meaning in the United States. But any historical account of the racialization of American education must avoid the easy familiarity of linear narrative. The reproduction of hegemonic racial meanings, the persistence of racial inequality and the mobilization of minority resistance to dominant educational institutions have not proceeded in a linear, coherent or predictable way. A systematic exploration of the history of race relations in education does, however, lead us to a recognition of the agency of oppressed minorities, the fluidity and complexity of social dynamics and the many-sided character of minority/majority relations in education.

The tensions and silences within mainstream and radical approaches to racial inequality discussed here underscore the need for a more relational and contextual approach to the operation of racial differences in schooling. Such an approach would allow us to understand better the complex operation of racial logics in schooling and would help us to explore more adequately the vital links that exist between racial inequality and other dynamics — such as class and gender — operating in the school setting. In the next section, I will present two related alternative approaches — the theories of *parallelism* and *nonsynchrony* — that will directly address the conceptually difficult but intriguing issues concerning (a) the structuration and formation of racial difference in education, and (b) the intersection of race, class and gender dynamics in the institutional setting of schools.

Nonsynchrony and Parallelism: Linking Race to Gender and Class Dynamics in Education

Racial inequality is indeed a complex, many-sided phenomenon that embraces both structural and cultural characteristics. But exactly how does racial difference operate in education? How are the 'widely disparate circumstances of individual and group racial identities' (Omi and Winant, 1986, p. 169) intertwined and mediated in the formal and informal practices of social institutions such as schools? How do educational institutions 'integrate' the macro- and microdynamics of difference? One of the most significant contributions to an understanding of these difficult questions regarding the operation of racial inequality has been advanced by Apple and Weis (1983) in what they call the 'parallelist position'. Since the parallelist position not only represents a paradigm shift in the way contemporary curriculum theorists conceptualize race, but directly anticipates my reformulation of race relations in schooling, it is necessary to describe the theory in some detail.

Apple and Weis (1983) criticize the tendency of mainstream and radical theorists to bifurcate society into separate domains of structure and culture. They argue that such arbitrary bifurcation directly informs tendencies toward essentialism (single-cause explanations) in contemporary thinking about race. Researchers often 'locate the fundamental elements of race, not surprisingly, on their homeground' (Omi and Winant, 1986, p. 52). For neo-Marxists, then, it is necessary first to understand the class basis of racial inequality; and for liberal theorists, cultural and social values and prejudices are the primary sources of racial antagonism. In contrast, Apple and Weis contend that race is not a 'category' or a 'thing–in–itself' (Thompson, 1966), but a vital social process which is integrally linked to other social processes and dynamics operating in education and society. These proponents of the parallelist position therefore hold that at least *three* dynamics — class, race and gender — are essential in understanding schools and other institutions. None are reducible to the others, and class is not necessarily primary:

> A number of elements or dynamics are usually present at the same time in any one instance. This is important. Ideological form is *not* reducible to class. Processes of gender, age, and race enter directly into the ideological moment . . . It is actual-ly out of the articulation with, clash among, or contradictions among and within, say class, race, and sex that ideologies are lived in one's day-to-day life. (Apple and Weis, 1983, p. 24)

In addition to this critique of class essentialism, Apple and Weis (1983) also offer a re-evaluation of economically reductive explana-tions of unequal social relations. They acknowledge that the economy plays a powerful role in determining the structure of opportunities and positions in capitalist society, but in their view, 'the' economy does not exhaust all existing social relations in society. Rather than using the economy to explain everything, these theorists have argued for an enlarged view of the social formation in which the role of ideology and culture is recognized as integral to the shaping of un-equal social relations and life chances. Apple and Weis (1983) maintain that there are three spheres of social life: economic, political and cultural. These, too, are in continual interaction and are, in essence, arenas in which class, race and gender dynamics operate. Unlike adherents to base-superstructure models, these proponents of parallel-ist theory assume that action in one arena can have an effect on action in another. The parallelist position therefore presents us with a theory of *overdetermination* in which the unequal processes and outcomes of teaching and learning and of schooling in general are produced by constant interactions among three dynamics (race, gender and class) and in three spheres (economic, political and cultural). The parallelist model, taken from Apple and Weis (1983, p. 25), is presented in Figure 5.1.

The proposition that 'each sphere of social life is constituted of dynamics of class, race, and gender' (Apple and Weis, 1983, p. 25) has

Figure 5.1   The parallelist model

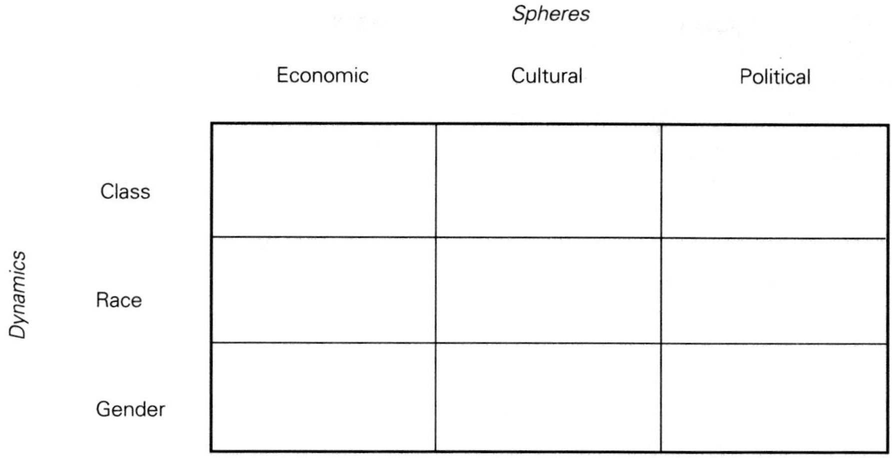

Spheres

	Economic	Cultural	Political
Class			
Race			
Gender			

Dynamics

Source: Michael W. Apple and Lois Weis (Eds), *Ideology and Practice in Schooling* (Philadelphia: Temple University Press, 1983), p. 25.

broad theoretical and practical merit. For example, it highlights the fact that it is impossible to understand fully the problem of the phenomenally high school dropout rate among black and Hispanic youth without taking into account the lived experience of race, class and gender oppressions in US urban centers and the ways in which the intersections of these social dynamics work to systematically 'disqualify' inner-city minority youth in educational institutions and in the job market. In a similar manner, a theoretical emphasis on gender dynamics complements our understanding of the unequal division of labor in schools and society and directs our attention to the way in which capitalism uses patriarchal relations to depress the wage scale and the social value of women's labor.

At a time when class-essentialist explanations still play such an important role in our thinking about schools and society, this movement toward a more relational or parallelist framework is to be welcomed. Increasingly, the work of feminist researchers in education, who argue that gender, race and class are irreducible dynamics and that each must be taken equally seriously, is being looked upon more favorably by other radical theorists (Apple and Beyer, 1988; Grant, 1984; Roman, Christian-Smith and Ellsworth, 1988). Even somewhat more economistic theorists have begun to recognize how important it is to deal more thoroughly with cultural and political power and conflict within state institutions (Carnoy and Levin, 1985).

There has been greater recognition, as well, of the efficacy of non-class social movements and movements that cut across class, gender and race lines, in the formation of social and educational policy. Thus the parallelist theoretical framework has proven to be a much more synthetic appraisal of how power operates than earlier accounts.

This does not mean, however, that the thesis of parallelism is without its problems. While I wish to support the validity of this model of interactions as expressing the character of the US formation at a very abstract level of generalization, there are limitations to this 'symmetrical' model at somewhat lower levels of abstraction (i.e., when applied to concrete institutional settings) that have been noted by writers such as Hicks, 1981, and Sarup, 1986. I will identify some of the problems with this formulation and suggest an alternative way of thinking about the operation of race and other dynamics is institutional settings.

First, it has become clear that at a conjunctural level of analysis, the parallelist model has not been adequate. It is often too general and loses cogency and specificity when applied to the actual operation of race, class and gender in institutional settings such as schools and classrooms. While the model does serve to make us stop and think about a broader range of dynamics and spheres than before, it is difficult to account for the various twists and turns of social and political life at the microlevel if our application of theory in inappropriately 'pitched' at too high a level of abstraction (Hall, 1986).

Second, this model unfortunately has often been construed in a static and simplistically additive way. Attempts to specify the dynamics of raced, classed and gendered phenomena in education are often formulated in terms of a system of linear 'additions' or gradations of oppression (Sarup, 1986). Thus, for example, Spencer (1984), in her insightful case study of women school teachers, draws attention to their double oppression. Simply put, these women performed onerous tasks with respect to both their domestic and emotional labor in the home and their instructional labor in the classroom (pp. 283–96). In Spencer's analysis, the oppression of these women in the home is 'added' to their oppression as female teachers working in the classroom. No attempt is made here to represent the *qualitatively* different experiences of patriarchy that black women encounter in their daily lives, both in the context of the domestic sphere and within the teaching profession itself. In this essentially incremental model of oppression, patriarchal and class forms of oppression unproblematically reproduce each other. Accounts of the intersection of race, class and gender such as these overlook instances of tension, contradiction and discontinuity in the institutional life of the school setting (McCarthy and Apple, 1988). In addition, the parallelist position does not fully address the 'mix' of contingencies, interests, needs, differential assets and capacities in the local setting such as the school. Dynamics of race, class and gender are conceptualized as having individual and uninterrupted effects.

Notions of double and triple oppression are not wholly inaccurate, of course. However, we need to see these relations as far more complex, problematic and contradictory than is suggested by parallelist theory. One of the most useful attempts to conceptualize the interconnections among race, class and gender has been formulated by Emily Hicks (1981). She cautions critical researchers against the tendency to theorize the interrelations among social dynamics as 'parallel', 'reciprocal' or 'symmetrical'. Instead, Hicks offers the thesis that the operation of race, class and gender relations at the level of daily practices in schools, workplaces, etc., is systematically *contradictory* or *nonsynchronous*. Hick's emphasis on nonsynchrony helps to lay the basis for an alternative approach to thinking about these social relations and dynamics at the institutional level.

By invoking the concept of nonsynchrony, I wish to advance the position that individuals or groups, in their relation to economic, political and cultural institutions such as schools, do *not* share identical consciousness and express the same interests, needs or desires 'at the same point in time' (Hicks, 1981, p. 221). In this connection, I also attach great importance to the organizing principles of selection, inclusion and exclusion. These principles operate in ways that affect how marginalized minority youth are positioned in dominant social and educational policies and agendas. Schooling in this sense constitutes a site for the production of politics. The politics of difference is a critical dimension of the way in which nonsynchrony operates in the material context of the school and can be regarded as the expression of 'culturally sanctioned, rational responses to struggles over scarce [or unequal] resources' (Wellman, 1977, p. 4). As we will see, students (and teachers) tend to be rewarded and sanctioned differently according to the resources and assets they are able to mobilize inside the school and in the community. This capacity to mobilize resources and to exploit the unequal reward system and symbolic rituals of schooling varies considerably according to the race, gender and class backgrounds of minority and majority students. White middle-class male students therefore come into schools with clear social and economic advantages and in turn often have these advantages confirmed and augmented by the unequal curriculum and pedagogical practices of schooling. However, this process is not simple, and the production of inequality in school is a highly contradictory and nonsynchronous phenomenon — one that does not guarantee nice, clean or definitive outcomes for embattled minority and majority school actors.

But exactly how does nonsynchrony work in practice? What are the 'rules of the game' that govern the production of inequality in the school setting? And how does inequality in educational institutions become specifically classed, gendered or raced?

There are four types of relations that govern the nonsychronous interactions of raced, classed and gendered minority and majority actors in the school setting. These relations can be specified as follows:

1   *Relations of competition*: These include competition for access to educational institutions, credentials, instructional opportunity, financial and technical resources and so on.
2   *Relations of exploitation*: The school mediates the economy's demands for different types of labor in its preparation of school youth for the labor force.
3   *Relations of domination*: Power in schooling is highly stratified and is expressed in terms of a hierarchy of relations and structures — administration to teacher, teacher to student and so forth. The school also mediates demands for symbolic control and legitimation from a racial and patriarchal state.
4   *Relations of cultural selection*: This is the totalizing principle of 'difference' that organizes meaning and identity-formation in school life. This organizing principle is expressed in terms of cultural strategies or rules of inclusion/exclusion or in-group/ out-group that determine whose knowledge gets into the curriculum, and that also determine the pedagogical practices of ability grouping, diagnosing and marking of school youth. These relations also help to define the terms under which endogenous competition for credentials, resources and status can take place in the school. It should be noted that there is considerable overlap between and among the relations of cultural selection and the other relations of competition, exploitation and domination operating in the everyday practices of minority and majority school actors.

In the school setting, each of these four types of relations interacts with, defines and is defined by the others in an uneven and decentered manner. For example, the principles of cultural selection embodied in codes of dress, behavior and so forth, which help to determine the assignment of minority youth to low-ability groups (Grant, 1985; Rist, 1970), also help to position these youth in respect to power (domination) relations with majority peers and adults. Cultural selection therefore influences minority access to instructional opportunity as well as access to opportunities for leadership and status in the classroom and in the school (Gamoran and Berends, 1986). In a similar manner, relations of cultural selection help to regulate endogenous competition for credentials and resources, thereby constraining minority and majority students to a differential structure of 'choices' with respect to the job market and ultimately to the differential exploitation of their labor power by employers. Of course, the reverse is also true in that teachers' and administrators' perceptions of the structure of opportunities for minorities (exploitation relations) can have a significant impact on the processes of cultural selection of minority and majority students to ability groups and curricular tracks in schooling (Sarup, 1986; Spring, 1985; Troyna and Williams, 1986). By virtue of the operation of these four types of relations — of competition, exploitation, domination and cultural selection — and their complex interaction with dynamics of race, class and gender, schooling is a nonsynchronous situation or context. In this nonsynchronous context, racial dynamics constantly shape and are in turn shaped by the other forms of structuration, namely, gender and class (Brown, 1985).

The concept of nonsynchrony begins to get at the complexity of causal motion and effects 'on the ground', as it were. It also raises questions about the nature, exercise and multiple determination of power within that middle ground of everyday practices in schooling (Scott and Kerkvliet, 1986). The fact is that, as Hicks (1981) suggests, dynamic relations of race, class and gender do not unproblematically reproduce each other. These relations are complex and often have contradictory effects in institutional settings. The intersection of race, class and gender at the local level of schooling can lead to interruptions, discontinuities, augmentations or diminutions of the original effects of any one of these dynamics. Thus, for example, while schooling in a racist society like the US is by definition a 'racist institution' (Carmichael and Hamilton, 1967), its racial character might not be the dominant variable shaping conflict over inequality in every schooling situation. That is to say that (a) the particular mix of history, subjectivities, interests and capacities that minority and majority actors bring to the institutional context, and (b) the way in which these actors negotiate and 'settle' the rules of the game (the relations of

85

competition, exploitation, domination and cultural selection) will determine the dominant character and directionality of effects in the specific school setting.

Such a 'dominant' character refers to the relations along which 'endogenous differences' in the school are principally articulated. These dominant relations thus constitute an 'articulating principle' (Laclau and Mouffe, 1982, 1985), pulling the entire ensemble of relations in the school setting into a 'unity' or focus for conflict. Such an articulating principle may be race, class or gender. For instance, it can be argued that a sex-dominant situation exists within American university education with respect to struggles over women's studies and the very status of women in academe itself. Gender has been the articulating principle that has sharpened our focus on issues around the fundamental white male privilege operating in the university system with respect to the differentiated organization of curricular knowledge, unequal patterns of selection and appointment to tenure-track faculty positions, unequal relations between male professors and female students, and so on. The issue of gender has had multiplier effects, illuminating flash points of difference across a range of traditional male-dominated disciplines. Sexual antagonism within academe has focused our attention on the *modus operandi* of the university and its relations of competition, exploitation, domination and cultural selection.

The powerful impact of sexual antagonism within the university has also had the effect of masking racial antagonism and or determining the political terms on which racial conflicts may be fought. (One should hasten to note that the opposite was true in the 1960s, when the balance of forces of contestation tended toward the prominence of racial difference as the articulating principle for conflicts over inequality in education.) Issues of minority failure and the under-representation of minorities at every level within the tertiary section of American education continue to be peripheral to the dominant Anglo-centric agenda in the university system. Figure 5.2 illustrates the interaction of race, gender and class relations in a sex-dominant situation. In this model of nonsynchrony, relations of sexual antagonism and solidarity are augmented while race and class relations are diminished. The principal sources of conflict, mobilization and counter-mobilization within given educational institutions may then be around issues concerning gender relations: sexual harassment, women's studies, new codes of conduct within the university with regards to relations among the sexes and so forth. This might not necessarily mean that issues around race are totally ignored. Indeed, one result might be that issues concerning minority women and their interests and aspirations would become more directly strategic and pivotal in the overall effort to secure reform in race relations in education — a situation in which it could be said that race-relations struggles in education benefited from a highly augmented focus on issues concerning gender. (Clearly the reverse was true in the 1960s.)

Within the current sociological and educational literature, there are a number of practical examples of the contradictory effects of the intersection of race, class and gender in settings inside and outside schools that can help to illustrate the nonsynchronous model I have outlined.

The work of researchers such as Omi and Winant (1986) and Sarup (1986) directs our attention to the issues of nonsynchrony and contradiction in minority/majority relations in education and society and suggests not only their complexity but the impossibility of predicting the effects of these dynamic relations in any formulaic way based on a monolithic view of race. In their discussion of educational and political institutions, Omi and Winant and Sarup have emphasized the fact that racial and sexual antagonisms can, at times, 'cut at right angles to class solidarity'.

The work of Marable (1985) and Spring (1985) focuses our attention in the opposite direction by pointing to the way in which class antagonisms have tended to undermine racial solidarity among minority groups involved in mainstream institutions. For instance, Marable and Spring argue that since the civil rights gains of the 1960s, there has been a powerful socioeconomic and cultural division within the African American community. This has been principally expressed in terms of the evolution of an upwardly mobile black middle class which has sought to distance itself in social, educational and political terms from an increasingly impoverished black underclass. Spring contends that such class antagonism operates as a determining variable in critical relationships between the black community and mainstream educational institutions. As we shall see, such class antagonism also influences and is vitally influenced by the endogenous relations of differentiation already existing within the school setting.

As a case in point, Spring (1985) reports on a longitudinal study of the class dynamics operating within a black suburban community ('Black Suburbia') and the way in which these dynamics get expressed in the relationship of black students and their parents to the school system. Spring's account begins in the mid-1960s, when a black professional middle-class (PMC) population moved into a midwestern suburb, formerly populated predominantly by whites. The new resi-

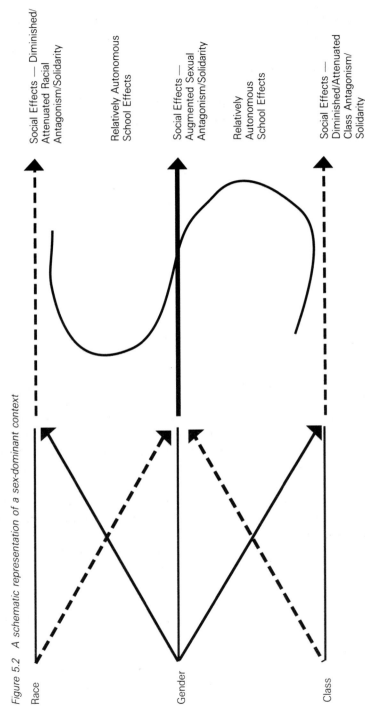

Figure 5.2 A schematic representation of a sex-dominant context

A schematic representation of the intersection of dynamics of race, gender, and class in schooling (S), in which gender is responsible for the most powerful effects in the school setting.
Strong lines indicate autonomous effects.
Double strong lines indicate augmented effects.
Broken lines indicate attenuated/relatively autonomous or diminished effects.

dents of Black Suburbia quickly embraced the predominantly white-administered school system. As the constituents of the 'new' middle class in the district, black PMC parents and their children readily granted legitimacy to the existing relations of differentiation (cultural selection, competition and so forth) operating in the schools in exchange for access to 'quality education'. They saw the schools as guarantors of continued upward mobility for their children. According to Spring:

> A study of the community [Black Suburbia] in the late 1960s showed the mobility concerns and educational aspirations of the new black population ... The study found that both the middle-aged and young middle-class black residents had high expectations of upward mobility and believed that *quality* schools were a major element in *quality* community. The population group labeled 'New, Middle-Aged, Black Middle-Class Residents' were earning more than $10,000 a year and were employed as managers, proprietors, and professionals. This group was found to have an 'extraordinarily high degree' of expectations for continuing upward mobility and concern about the quality of schools. (Spring, 1985, pp. 105–6)

The term 'quality school' indeed summarized an ideological and strategic trade-off or 'settlement' that was tacitly implicated in the overwhelming black PMC support for the white-administered school system. But this settlement between the school system and its new PMC patrons was soon to be imperiled by a change in the demographic and cultural milieu of the Black Suburbia community and its schools. And both the expectations of upward mobility and the high educational aspirations of the black PMC residents who had arrived in the late 1960s were, by the 1970s, 'threatened by the rapid influx of a poor black population' (Spring, 1985, p. 106). This influx of low-income blacks dramatically altered the social class composition of Black Suburbia: 'Between 1970 and 1973 the percentage of children from welfare families increased ... from 16 to 51 percent. In other words, the migration of upwardly mobile middle-class blacks was followed by the rapid migration of black welfare families' (*ibid.*, p. 106).

Teachers responded negatively to the entrance of increased numbers of low-income black students into the school system and the 'standard of education' in Black Suburbia schools declined:

One of the first things to happen was that the educational expectations of the mainly white teachers and administrators in the school system began to fall. This seemed to be caused by the assumption of the white school staff that the blacks moving into the community were not interested in education and would create major problems in the school system. (Spring, 1985, p. 108)

These developments precipitated a crisis of legitimacy in the school system's relations to its black constituents. However, the racial response of the school system to black students was not met or challenged by a united front among the black residents of Black Suburbia. Indeed, class antagonism between the more affluent blacks and the lower class black residents intensified both in the schools and in the community. PMC black students blamed the lower class students for the sharp decline in educational standards in the schools. They complained that the teachers were incapable of controlling the 'rowdies' — a code word for low-income black students. This class antagonism spilled over into the community. Many black PMC parents expressed the fear that their children would be corrupted by the 'rowdy-culture' of welfare kids who 'were organized into natural street groupings', as one parent put it (Spring, 1985, p. 108). As class antagonism intensified, the more affluent black parents took the further step of withdrawing their children from the public schools and sending them to private institutions. To put the matter directly, black PMC parents lost confidence in the public schools because they perceived teachers as having failed to control the 'corrupting' influence of low-income students, whom these parents blamed along with their teachers for the declining standard of education.

From the perspectives of these PMC black residents, the Black Suburbia school system had failed to deliver on its side of a tacit agreement and black students stood to suffer in competitive relations for credentials and long-term futures in the labor market. According to Spring's account, the racially motivated strategies of cultural selection that obtained in the Black Suburbia schools, had, as a response to the influx of low-income students, now come full circle to handicap black middle-class youth as well. But ultimately, in this highly provocative racial situation, the response of the residents of Black Suburbia to their school system was highly contradictory and nonsynchronous. Racial dynamics and identity were clearly 'dominated' by class interests. To say the least, the interests of black PMC residents and their low-income counterparts diverged. Resulting class antagonism undermined racial solidarity among black residents and weakened their collective ability to negotiate with the white-administered school system or challenge the racial basis of the poor quality education that the public schools were offering to their children.

Nkomo (1984), in his discussion of the dynamics of race/class relations in the South African educational system, describes an example of a nonsynchronous racial situation. In this case, Nkomo asserts that the enormous constraints placed on the aspirations and economic futures of black students and the blatant Afrikaner ideological domination of black universities have had unintended effects nonsynchronous with the interests of the apartheid state. High levels of cultural alienation experienced in South African Bantu universities by both black students from urban PMC backgrounds and working-class students from the Bantustans have heightened the bonds of racial solidarity between these youth of different class backgrounds. But racial solidarity among black students is certainly not a policy goal of the South African government. Indeed, ever since the late 1950s, the South African government has sought to balkanize South African black youth by creating highly restrictive, ethnically segregated universities in the Bantustans. The Afrikaner regime has attempted to maintain existing relations of racial domination and exploitation of South African blacks by pursuing a policy of 'separate development' (Nkomo, 1984). In the area of higher education, this policy of balkanization has meant, for example, that student enrollment at the University of Zululand is limited exclusively to the Zulu and Swazi ethnic groups. And while, prior to the late 1950s, Indians and 'coloreds' could go to the University College of Fort Hare, the 1959 Transfer Act restricted enrollment at this college to Xhosa-speaking Africans only (Nkomo, 1984).

The clear intent of such divide-and-conquer policies of the South African government was to promote the intensification of intra- and inter-ethnic differences among Africans, Indians and 'coloreds' as a means of disorganizing the political capacities and the collective will of the subordinated racial groups in South Africa. But Nkomo informs us that the South African state's domination of black universities goes even further. Through the Department of Bantu Education, there is direct state control over the curriculum content, student admissions, academic staff appointments and finances of these black universities. This abnormal state control is peculiar to the Bantu universities, since the 'European' universities in South Africa enjoy academic autonomy in consonance with the western tradition.

But it is precisely this intense racialization of the South African state's relationship to the black universities and its coercive attempt to consolidate relations of domination in these educational institutions that have led to a radical incongruity between black students' aspirations and the official university establishment. These contradictions and frustrations within the apartheid Bantu educational system have provoked a critical consciousness among urban PMC black students and their less privileged counterparts from the Bantustans that has allowed them to band together in a common struggle against the apartheid system. This development is not without its touch of irony: Bantu universities created by the South African government as part of the apartheid structure and developed to facilitate exploitation by undermining political alliances among black South African youth have had the unintended effect of galvanizing powerful cultural resistance and racial solidarity against the apartheid system. Indeed, these Bantu universities have been among the principal sites of racial mobilization and struggle against apartheid in the 1980s and now in the 1990s.

The example of the black South African university is illustrative of a race-dominant nonsynchronous situation. As Nkomo (1984) demonstrates, racial solidarity and its obverse, racial antagonism, constitute the dominant principles along which unequal social relations in these Bantu universities are ordered, organized and culturally expressed — this, despite the significant economic and social class divides that exist among black South African students.

A final example gets us closer to the nonsynchronous dynamics of unequal social relations in a number of classrooms in the United States. Based on findings from a study of 'face-to-face interactions' in six desegregated elementary school classrooms in a midwestern industrial city, Linda Grant (1984) concludes that 'Black females' experiences in desegregated schools ... differ from those of other race-gender groups and cannot be fully understood ... by extrapolating from the research on females or research on blacks' (p. 99).

Grant (1984) conducted detailed observations of the classrooms of six teachers (all women, three blacks and three whites) at the two schools, Ridgeley and Glendon, involved in her two-year study. Some 40 per cent of the 139 students in the first-grade classrooms studied were black. Among other things, Grant found that strategies of evaluation and cultural selection (tracking, ability grouping and so forth) varied considerably according to 'race-gender group' (black males, black females, white females and white males). For instance, black females were more likely than any other race-gender group to be labeled 'non-academic' (p. 102). This was particularly true of the evaluations by white teachers:

White teachers, however, gave more attention to non-academic criteria. In fact, they made proportionally fewer comments of an academic nature about black girls than any other race-gender group. [For example,] assessments of black females contrasted markedly with these teachers' assessments of white males, for which academic criteria predominated . . . (p. 102)

While teachers identified both black and white females as more mature and 'helpful' than their male counterparts, white girls were more likely to be labeled as 'cognitively mature and ready for school' (Grant, 1984, p. 102). In contrast, black girls were labeled as 'socially mature', and Grant contends that teachers exploited this 'social maturity'. Teachers' strategies of cultural selection also had an impact on domination relations of teacher to student and student to student in these first-grade classrooms. Thus, teachers tended to deploy black girls as 'go-betweens' when they wanted to communicate rules and convey messages informally to black boys (p. 106). Race-gender group differences were also reproduced in terms of the first graders' access to instructional opportunity as well as in the students' informal relations and orientation to teachers in the Ridgeley and Glendon elementary schools:

Although generally compliant with teachers' rules, black females were less tied to teachers than white girls were and approached them only when they had a specific need to do so. White girls spent more time with teachers, prolonging questions into chats about personal issues. Black girls' contacts were briefer, more task related, and often on behalf of a peer rather than self. (Grant, 1984, p. 107)

Black males were even less likely than black females — or any other race-gender group — to have extended chats with teachers. And relations between black males and their female teachers were defined by mutual estrangement. Indeed, Grant suggests in another article based on the same data (Grant, 1985) that these teachers were afraid of or 'threatened' by their black male students. Nevertheless, teachers tended to identify at least one black male in each class whom they singled out as an academic achiever or a 'superstar'. In none of the six elementary school classrooms that Grant studied was any of the black girls singled out as a high academic achiever (Grant, 1984, p. 100). Instead, Grant maintains, black girls were typified as 'average

achievers' and assigned to 'average' or 'below average' track place-
ments and ability groups.

Ultimately, the effects of the processes of cultural selection that
obtained in the classrooms that Grant (1984) observed were nonsynchronous. Teachers did not relate to their black students or white
students in any consistent or monolithic way. Gender differences
powerfully influenced and modified the differential ways in which
teachers evaluated, assessed, diagnosed, labeled and tracked black and
white students. The influence of gender on the racial response of
teachers to their students was particularly evident in the case of black
females. In significant ways, teachers emphasized the social, caring
and nurturing qualities of the black females in their first-grade classrooms. In subtle ways, teachers encouraged 'black girls to pursue
social contacts, rather than press towards high academic achievement'
(p. 103). Consequently, Grant concludes that desegregated education
at the elementary schools she studied had unintended negative (racial)
costs for all black children. The processes of cultural selection that
obtained in the desegregated classrooms she observed worked to the
disadvantage of black children with respect to competition for instructional opportunity, teacher time and resources in these schools. Grant
also suggests that existing processes of cultural differentiation not only
served to constrain the structure of educational opportunity available
to black students within the school setting, but also helped to structure their incorporation into exploitation relations from the very start
of their school careers. For black females these costs were particularly
severe and were determined strongly by gender. This meant that
black girls' experiences in the six desegregated classrooms were systematically nonsynchronous or qualitatively different from those of
black boys or any other race-gender group:

> The emphasis on black girls' social rather than academic skills,
> which occurs particularly in white-teacher classrooms, might
> point to a hidden cost of desegregation for black girls.
> Although they are usually the top students in black classes,
> they lose this stature to white children in desegregated rooms.
> Their development seems to become less balanced, with em-
> phasis on social skills ... Black girls' everyday schooling
> experiences seem more likely to nudge them toward stereo-
> typical roles of black women than toward [academic] alterna-
> tives. These include serving others and maintaining peaceable
> ties among diverse persons rather than developing one's own
> skills. (Grant, 1984, p. 109)

Conclusion

The findings of curriculum and educational researchers such as Grant (1984, 1985), Nkomo (1984) and Spring (1985) help to illustrate and clarify the complex workings of racial logics in the highly differentiated environment that exists in school settings. By drawing attention to contradiction and nonsynchrony in educational processes of cultural selection, competition, exploitation and domination, these critical researchers directly challenge mainstream single-group studies of inequality in schooling that have tended to isolate the variable of race from gender and class. Instead, the work of Grant and others underscores the need to examine the historical specificity and variability of race and its nonsynchronous interaction with forms of class and gender structuration in education. Monolithic theories of racial inequality suppress such an understanding of these complexities and treat racial groups as biological and cultural 'unities' (Troyna and Williams, 1986).

The nonsynchronous approach to the study of inequality in schooling alerts us to the fact that different race-class-gender groups not only have qualitatively different experiences in schools, but actually exist in constitutive tension, often engage in active competition with each other, receive different forms of rewards, sanctions and evaluation, and are ultimately structured into differential futures. The critical theoretical and practical task, then, as Hall (1980) suggests, is one of 'radically decoding' the specific relations and nuances of particular historical and institutional contexts:

> One needs to know how different groups were inserted historically, and the relations which have tended to erode and transform, or to preserve these distinctions through time — not simply as residues and traces of previous modes, but as active structuring principles of the present society. Racial categories *alone* will *not* provide or explain these. (Hall, 1980, p. 339)

The work of Grant (1984), Nkomo (1984), Spring (1985) and Sarup (1986) has furthered our understanding of the complex workings of race and other dynamics in educational institutions. Their findings are also important in helping us to deconstruct the multiple determination of power in the school setting and the way in which such micropolitics can undermine the viability of conventional approaches to curriculum reform. What is abundantly clear is that monolithic or homogeneous strategies of curriculum reform that attempt to ignore or avoid the contradictions of race, class and gender at the institutional level will be of limited usefulness to minority youth. In the next and final chapter, I will look at current approaches to educational reform and discuss some of the basic principles of an alternative or nonsynchronous approach to racial inequality and educational change in the United States.

Chapter 6

Racial Inequality and the Challenge of Educational Reform

Theory and Practice

Radical and neo-Marxist theorists writing on social differences and inequality in education have often been assailed for being notoriously short on the specification of alternatives and programs that could make a difference in the educational lives of minorities and other oppressed groups. Conversely, mainstream educators have been criticized for paying little attention to theory and conceptual rigor in their formulations on schooling (Giroux, 1985). In part, this bifurcation is misleading. Both mainstream and radical school critics incorporate and address aspects of theory and practice in their writings on education. The tension between theory and practice in contemporary research on racial inequality does, however, bring into focus a far more consequential matter — that is, that the production of education theory and research is itself a site of ideological and political struggle. We can sometimes forget that within the corridors of the academy, oblique but often very significant struggles over credibility and ascendancy are constantly being waged within and between 'communities' of discourses on curriculum and education.

In this regard, mainstream conservative and liberal theorists have sought to appropriate the language of 'practice', 'practical', 'pragmatic' and so forth, to describe only what they do. 'Practice' in mainstream discourses has often meant the stipulation of 'workable' programs and policies designed for operation within the rules and terms of reference of existing institutional structures and the relations of competition, exploitation, domination and cultural selection that I described in the previous chapter. Practice in the mainstream sense at best merely allows for incremental modification necessary for the maintenance of existing institutional frameworks and power relations. Hence, the variety of special programs for 'at risk' youth, multicultural curricula and so forth, are, in this vein, products of liberal attempts to incorporate and redirect the demand of minorities and women for fundamental educational changes. These radical demands are then turned into 'functional', 'practical' and, ultimately, hegemonic educational policy. Some of these programs, such as multiculturalism, do show potential, but they almost remain unpoliticized. Such programs are not thoroughly enough linked to larger movements and political projects aimed at securing social change.

By contrast, radical theoretical work in education has sought to expose the limitations and oppressiveness that many existing educational arrangements, school curricula and differential resources impose on socially disadvantaged groups. Radical school critics have sought to link issues around curriculum and educational reform directly to strategies for fundamental changes in the social and economic structures of capitalist society (Bowles and Gintis, 1976; Freire, 1970, 1985; Giroux, 1985). This, then, is in a general sense part of the ideological vision that informs the practice of radical scholarship. As educators committed to the expansion of democracy in all its forms, we must never abandon the notion that committed theoretical work is itself a worthwhile, necessary and consequential *practice* — if and *only* if it is also linked to concrete attempts by real people in real institutions to create more democratic cultural, political and economic relations.

Having said this, however, it is important to recognize that radical theorists of education have been slow to address the actual formulation of policy and decision-making — precisely those areas of educational policy that liberal school critics have labeled as 'practical'. As Troyna and Williams (1986) have pointed out, the formulation of policy and decision-making within the state and the educational system constitutes a political process in which women, minorities and socially disadvantaged youth are processually disenfranchised and their interests and demands delegitimated. Troyna and Williams contend further that it is precisely in this area of decision-making, policy formulation and the development of the instrumental rules that define the institutional relations in schooling that left educators are too often outnumbered, outorganized and outmaneuvered.

But matters are never as clear-cut as this. As I showed in my discussion of the theoretical and conceptual issues concerning racial inequality, there is considerable contradiction, discontinuity and variability within contemporary research paradigms on race and education. This is no less the case with respect to educators' articulation of curriculum and educational reforms that address race relations in schooling. Mainstream and radical educators' approaches to educational reform in large measure reflect their conceptual predispositions and theoretical stances on racial inequality. As was the case with the theoretical discussion of race, both mainstream and radical proponents of educational reforms follow a decidedly ethnocentric path in their specification of what is to be done about minority disadvantage in schooling and society. On the one hand, mainstream liberal and neo-conservative educators fail to problematize dominant white values, modes of success and so on. Instead, they generally propose models of educational and social reforms that require minority integration, incorporation and uncritical participation in dominant society as preconditions for access to educational and social rewards. On the other hand, neo–Marxist approaches do not significantly integrate minority needs and interests into their proposals for educational change.

More important than the issue of ethnocentrism, however, is the fact that neither mainstream nor radical educators sufficiently take into account the issue of nonsynchrony and the differential capacities, needs and interests that define minority/majority relations in educational and social contexts. As we shall see in this chapter, current race-relations reforms in schooling, such as desegregation, are often subverted by the procedural discontinuities that result from the clash of nonsynchronous interests, needs and desires that separate various segments of minority groups from each other and minority actors from their majority counterparts in educational settings as well as in the larger society.

These criticisms aside, it should be acknowledged that current approaches to race and education do offer pertinent and strategically important directions for rethinking the issue of race-relations reform. In the first part of this chapter, I will discuss the limits and possibilities of current mainstream (liberal and neo-conservative) and radical proposals for reform in race relations in schooling. In the second part, I will offer some specifications of my own regarding a nonsynchronous approach to race-relations reforms that links the micropolitics of curriculum and institutional practices in schools to a broad-based politics for social emancipation. Such a nonsynchronous and expanded approach to race and educational change attaches pivotal importance to the differential needs and interests of minority men and women and urban, working–class youth.

Let us now look at how mainstream researchers and educators have addressed the issue of race and educational reform.

Mainstream Approaches to Race and Educational Reform

You will recall that in Chapter 2 I drew attention to discontinuities and tensions within mainstream theoretical frameworks on race and education. I summarized these differences by referring to the liberal versus conservative/neo-conservative branches of mainstream theories of education. I believe that these categorical distinctions are still quite useful for making sense of the inconsistencies and incongruities that one finds in reviewing mainstream approaches to race and educational reform. Simply put, the tensions that exist at a theoretical level are reproduced at the level of practical proposals for educational change. But before we discuss these programmatic and practical differences within mainstream approaches, it is necessary to briefly retrace some important theoretical ground.

There is a basic principle of instrumental reasoning that undergirds mainstream thinking on the function of education in a 'plural' society such as the United States. Mainstream theorists and educators generally insist that the primary role of educational institutions in this society must be that of facilitating the competititiveness of its economic institutions and the viability of its democratic forms (Ogbu and Matute-Bianchi, 1986). Correlative with this assertion, mainstream theorists also contend that the educational system offers to individuals the opportunity for personal success and rewards in return for effort and achievement (Hurn, 1979). The one complements the other: individual effort, ingenuity and success provide the motor of a healthy capitalist system, and the latter in turn offers the individual opportunities for social rewards and mobility. It is, however, generally acknowledged that not all individuals are successful in procuring capitalism's rewards and that black and other minority youth are disproportionately more likely than majority whites to be unsuccessful in the educational system (Hurn, 1979; Troyna and Williams, 1986). Indeed, current statistics on inequality, which I presented earlier, make it abundantly clear that poverty and educational 'underachievement' among blacks,

Hispanics and Native Americans have reached crisis proportions as we enter the 1990s.

As I also indicated in Chapter 2, liberal and conservative theorists differ significantly in their specification of the 'causes' of minority 'failure'. While both liberals and conservatives locate minority disadvantage in specific minority deficits such as 'the black family' (Moynihan, 1965), liberal thinkers have tended to offer more 'enlightened' explanations of these disadvantages. Thus liberal theorists, from Myrdal (1944) to current proponents of multiculturalism such as Banks (1981, 1987), have argued that these minority deficits are socially based and that, in addition, racial prejudice and discriminatory practices perpetrated by majority individuals constrain minority chances in education and in the job market. In contrast, conservative educators have tended to offer more restrictive explanations of minority disadvantage. Conservatives insist instead that certain genetic and, more recently (with neo-conservatives such as Bloom, 1987), cultural characteristics endogenous and particular to given minority groups inhibit the educational and life chances of individuals from these groups (Sowell, 1981; Steele, 1989). These differences among mainstream theorists with respect to the 'causes' of minority disadvantage are also expressed in liberal and conservative 'solutions' to the problem of racial inequality in education and society.

Reformism: The Liberals

Over the last three decades or so, liberal sociologists of education, curriculum theorists and policy intellectuals such as Bloom, Davis and Hess (1965), Jacob (1988) and Moynihan (1965) have directed significant reformist efforts at making the case for expanding the base of educational and social opportunity available to minorities as American citizens. These reformist efforts have been built around the central assumption that the state is neutral and open to rational arguments. Liberals feel that racism based in prejudice and misunderstanding is ultimately reversible and eradicable if state-controlled institutions such as schools take appropriate action to eliminate prejudice and guarantee equality of opportunity. In addition, liberal educators such as Bloom, Davis and Hess (1965) and Tiedt and Tiedt (1986) have made the case for compensatory education policies that would directly address the special needs of 'culturally deprived' inner-city youth.

Policy positions of liberal educators and social theorists have directly informed wide-ranging programs in race-relations reform in education in the following areas:

a) federal and state legislative and monetary initiatives with respect to such programs as compensatory education (Head Start, Upward Bound), desegregation and so on;
b) local and school-based efforts to extend equality of opportunity to minorities by increasing minority representation on school faculty and in educational administration;
c) curricular reform emphasizing multicultural and bilingual education and the wider inclusion of minority history, language and achievement in textbooks and other curricular materials.

But the heyday of the liberal reformist offensive in race relations was the 1960s. The grand achievement of the liberal reformers and policy intellectuals was that they were able to contribute significantly to the building of a moral 'consensus' within the state for ameliorative action in race relations in education and society. Such militant centrism created a *via media* between the radical cultural nationalist and separatist demands articulated by some sections of contending minority groups and the rearguard action of conservatives directed at limiting educational and social reform in race relations. Although the impact of such reformist measures has been mixed, there have been demonstrable benefits, particularly with respect to expanding opportunities for minorities in education and employment (notably at the lower and middle levels of the public sector). Indeed, the partial ventilation of economic positions in American society that took place in the 1960s (the 'Great Transformation', as Omi and Winant, 1986, would call it) laid the basis for the emergence of a new black middle class (Marable, 1985; Spring, 1985).

But the impact of ameliorative programs has been experienced differentially within minority communities. Internal class differences in capacity, assets and access to education and credentials among members of particular minority groups have effectively determined who would benefit most from liberal ameliorative policies (Crichlow, 1990). Ironically, while the black middle class can point to identifiable social and economic gains, liberal reformism has failed to deliver in the same measure to the most disenfranchised class of minorities — the urban and inner-city poor who have been overwhelmed by a worsening capitalist economy, systematic de-industralization and the attendent loss of jobs and infrastructure that support the urban centers in the United States (Crichlow, 1990). These developments and the uneven, differential and nonsynchronous effects of the incipient fiscal crisis have helped to set the stage for a popular rejection of liberal reformism in the 1990s and the emergence of new intellectual and political currents in American education in the form of a new conservative movement. The impact of neo-conservatism on the state, educational thinking and race relations has been significant. I would now like to turn to a discussion of neo-conservative approaches to racial inequality and educational reform.

Reformism: The New Conservatives

A new economic division pits the producers — business, manufacturers, hard-hats, blue-collar workers and farmers — against a new and powerful class of non-producers comprised of a liberal verbalist elite (the dominant media, the major foundations and research institutions, the educational establishment, the federal and state bureaucracies) and a semi-permanent welfare constituency, all coexisting happily in a state of mutually sustaining symbiosis. (Rusher, 1975, p. 31)

Neo-conservative thinking in education represents part of a broad-based popular disaffection with liberal reformism and its encouragement of state-sponsored programs and policies aimed at the amelioration of racial inequality and disadvantage experienced by minority groups. This neo-conservative critique of liberal reformism has been in large measure bolstered by the ascendancy of conservative US administrations in the 1980s and 1990s, which have initiated a steady retreat from the progressive gains of the 1960s in such areas as affirmative action, bilingual education and desegregation. This neo-conservative offensive has involved a strategic rearticulation of such civil rights themes as 'equality of opportunity' and 'racial justice' (Omi and Winant, 1986, p. 129). In this discourse, white Americans, particularly white males, are seen as the new victims of 'reverse discrimination' generated by misguided state policies that favor minorities. These developments highlight the powerful effects of nonsynchronous differences that currently exist within the American working class. The racialization of popular discourses over educational and social reform brings into the foreground the issue of working-class solidarity and the way in which such solidarity remains vulnerable to the effects of nonsynchronous interests and identities that systematically undermine the possibility of alliances between black and white workers even in these hard economic times. But neo-conservative approaches to race relations reform also foreground profound and disturbing effects of nonsynchrony within minority communities themselves. For example, significant class differences within the black community have been expressed in terms of a cultural alienation of the black middle class from the values and attitudes associated with minority underclasses. Nowhere is this nonsynchronous class tension more powerfully expressed than in black intellectual discourses on the issue of minority underachievement in schooling.

A very good example of this neo-conservative trend in black scholarship on minority disadvantage is illustrated in the writings of Shelby Steele (1989). In a recent essay entitled 'The Recoloring of Campus Life', Steele draws the line for a neo-conservative stand against black charges of persistent institutional racism on college campuses. He points to an idyllic past in the university setting, when black students strove for academic success despite severe social and economic constraints. White students were supportive or unobtrusive and blacks achieved their goals in intellectual and cultural life. 'These days', things have changed for the worse because today's black students willfully squander the gains of previous generations by their preoccupation with public bantering, political ritual and exaggerated claims about white victimization of blacks. For Steele, both racial tension and minority underachievement in education are the results 'more of racial equality than inequality' (1989, p. 48). The problem of race in contemporary life, then, is a problem of changed attitudes among black students who no longer trust white officials and white students, and attend universities in bad faith:

> Of course universities are not where racial problems tend to arise. When I went to college in the mid-Sixties, colleges were oases of calm and understanding in a racially tense society; campus life — with its traditions of tolerance and fairness, its very distance from the 'real' world — imposed a degree of broad-mindedness on even the most provincial students. If I met whites who were not anxious to be friends with blacks, most were at least vaguely friendly to the cause of our freedom. In any case, there was no guerrilla activity against our presence, no 'mine field of racism' (as one black student at Berkeley recently put it) to negotiate. I wouldn't say that the phrase 'campus racism' is a contradiction in terms, but until

recently it certainly seemed an incongruence. (Steele, 1989, p. 48)

The ideas of writers such as Steele have become more prominent in educational theory and policy on race relations, and neo-conservatism has brought about a peculiar alliance between black and white conservatives. White neo-conservative intellectuals such as Bloom (1987) and Hirsch (1987) and black petty bourgeois social theorists such as Patterson (1977) and Sowell (1981) pursue similar lines of argument with respect to the issue of racial differences in education. These writers maintain that there must be a reordering of priorities in educational agendas. They insist, for instance, on the privileging of the goal of academic excellence over efforts to promote equity. Neo-conservatives (both black and white) have also argued vociferously for 'color-blind' educational policies and against the ethnicization of mainstream culture and the university curriculum. For example, Patterson (1977) maintains the following:

It was ridiculously easy for the [liberal] establishment to respond by changing the color of a few faces in the ads for the 'Pepsi generation,' by introducing a few network shows in which the traditional role of blacks as clowns and maids was updated (with the added boon that these new 'soul' shows have been extremely profitable), by publishing a spate of third-rate books on the greatness of the African tradition, by the glorification of black roots, and most cruel of all, by introducing into the curriculum of the nation's colleges that strange package of organized self-delusion which goes by the name of Afro-American studies. Black American ethnicity has encouraged the worst sociological problems of the group and an incapacity to distinguish the things that are worthwile in black life from those that are just plain rotten. (p. 155)

These neo-conservative fears of the corrosive effects of 'ethnicization' and the 'politics of difference' on educational life are also expressed in the writings of Steele (1989): 'Black studies departments, black deans of student affairs, black counseling programs, Afro houses, black theme houses, black homecoming dances and graduation ceremonies — black students and white administrators have slowly engineered a machinery of separatism that, in the name of sacred difference, redraws the ugly lines of segregation' (p. 55).

In brief, then, neo-conservatives contend that the state and educational institutions have been unduly compromised. They argue that liberal welfarist policies, though well-meaning, have had the unintentional effect of discouraging effort and achievement among minority youth. These social theorists and educators have therefore made the case for a new agenda in education and race relations for the 1990s and beyond. This new agenda emphasized the following:

1   An end to state-sponsored preferences to minorities as exemplified in such misguided policies as affirmative action (Loury, 1985; Sowell, 1975; Steele, 1989). For example, Bloom (1987) asserts: 'Affirmative action now institutionalizes the worst aspects of separatism. The fact is that the average black student's achievements do not equal those of the average white student in the good universities, and everybody knows it. It is also a fact that the university degree of a black student is also tainted, and employers look on it with suspicion, or become guilty accomplices in the toleration of incompetence' (Bloom, 1987, p. 96). Black neo-conservative intellectuals such as Sowell (1981) have argued that the end of the policy of perferential treatment to minorities in education and its replacement by a policy that grants rewards based on a system of merit would in turn stimulate effort and excellence among minority youth.

2   An end to the steady dilution of the school curriculum by the infusion of politically motivated subject matter such as ethnic studies and multicultural education. In a time when the American economy has declined relative to the economies of its international competitors, such as Japan, neo-conservatives have pointed to the failures of the educational system and the effete nature of present-day school curricula as explanations for 'why we have fallen behind' (Hirsch, 1987).

3   The reintroduction in American schools of a rigorous, academically-oriented core curriculum that stresses desirable aesthetic, social, intellectual and moral values that are best exemplified in the history, philsosphy, literature and scientific achievements of 'western culture' (Bloom, 1987; Hirsch, 1987).

4   The introduction of state-instituted programs that require minority underclasses to 'work' rather than to rely on 'handouts'. Solutions to the problems of poverty and educational underachievement and disadvantage will be possible only

when there are 'positive' attitudinal and cultural changes among the minority poor, and only when those most prone to being on welfare begin to pull themselves up by their boot-straps (Murray, 1984).

Many of these neo-conservative arguments have already been incorporated into policy proposals at the federal, state and local levels of educational administration and decision-making. These arguments have also been central to the language and ideological orientation of recent national reports on the state of education in America, such as the National Commission on Excellence in Education's *A Nation at Risk* (1983). These neo-conservative currents within government policy have, in the past few years, directly influenced the drive for greater 'accountability' in education, for state mandates directed at raising 'standards' and 'competence', and for a new approach to prioritization in education that privileges the needs of the economy over minority demands for equality (Apple and Beyer, 1988).

Although often couched as a 'return' to 'tradition', neo-conservatism therefore represents a whole new stance within main-stream thinking about race and educational reform. Both mainstream liberal and neo-conservative thinkers emphasize the role of education in reducing the effects of cultural deviance among minority groups, but neo-conservatives reject the programmatic status that liberal refor-mers have given to minority demands for equality in education and the social responsibility that liberals have assigned to the state in these matters. On the other hand, liberal reformers have argued for a central role for the state in addressing racial inequality and suggest that policies supporting or promoting equality of educational opportunity can help boost minority life-chances in American society.

As I have already suggested, it is impossible to ignore the critical role of neo-conservative elements within the black middle class, as represented by intellectuals such as Patterson, Sowell and Steele, who have lent 'legitimacy from below' (Simpson, 1987, p. 164) to the white backlash against the liberal consensus that earlier helped to realize real gains for minorities in education and elsewhere. In many respects, neo-conservative black intellectuals represent the clearest manifestation of nonsynchronous structural and cultural differentiation taking place within the black community in the 1990s. In underlining their class credentials and their nonsynchronous relationship to the black working class, these neo-conservative middle-class black school critics have lent powerful intellectual and political support to white conservatives and their efforts to reverse the ameliorative race-relations policies put in place in the 1960s. On the issue of educational reform, these school critics have vociferously expressed the idea that the time has come for minorities to abandon the role of 'victim' by taking full responsibility for their own futures in American society (Steele, 1989).

As we shall see in the next section, neo-Marxist and radical theorists are skeptical of mainstream liberal and neo-conservative approaches to race and educational reform. Such approaches, radical theorists argue, merely help to insulate existing capitalist relations of domination in American society from the kind of structual transformation that is necessary if the social well-being of minority underclasses is to be significantly improved (Edari, 1984).

Neo-Marxists and Educational Reform

> Educational reformers commonly err by treating the system of schools as if it existed in a social vacuum. (Bowles and Gintis, 1976, p. 256)

Though neo-Marxist educators offer powerful and compelling critiques of mainstream policy positions on race and educational change, these radical school critics are less than forthcoming when it comes to offering explicit policies and programs that could help to ameliorate the educational and social disadvantages experienced by minorities. Part of the explanation for this lack of specificity on race relations reform has first of all to do with the sober political reality of the systematic marginalization of radical discourses within the public domain. Second, racial antagonism has simply not been accorded the kind of theoretical or programmatic status within radical neo-Marxist frameworks that has been procedurally accorded to class. These matters aside, however, neo-Marxists do offer general proposals for educational and social change that are quite germane to the issue of race-relations reform in education.

Radical proposals for educational and social change divide along 'structural' and 'cultural' lines — a feature of radical accounts of inequality to which I drew attention in Chapter 4 when I discussed the conceptual and theoretical differences that currently exist in neo-Marxist frameworks. Briefly, structuralist approaches to educational reform are 'production driven' in that they consistently privilege class struggles in the workplace and the political party — over, say, ethnic/

racial struggles over schooling and declining community services in the inner city — as the preferred sites for the location of organizational and mobilizational challenges to capitalism. In a related sense, race relations are also seen as an extension of capital-labor relations, and it is felt that transformation of the latter would deprive racism of its material base and would eventually lead to the disappearance of racial and ethnic particularism. On the other hand, culturalist theorists, particularly critical curriculum theorists such as Wood (1985), maintain that struggles over capitalism are profoundly ideological in nature and centrally involve contestation within institutions such as schools over issues of meaning, language and cultural identity. Critical curriculum theorists also suggest that transformation of oppressive race, class and gender relations in schooling is an autonomous matter of no less importance in the overall project of socialist transformation than emancipatory actions in the workplace. But let us examine neo-Marxist perspectives on race-relations reform in more detail by first looking at the structuralist approach to this issue.

The Structuralists

Neo-Marxist structuralist educators generally disagree with the central tenet of neo-conservative thinking on education — that is, that 'social equality can be purchased only at the expense of economic efficiency' (Bowles and Gintis, 1976, p. 268). At the same time, these structuralist theorists express pessimism about liberal reformism in race relations in education. They argue that liberal thinking on educational change stops far short of addressing the structural relations of exploitation and domination that determine inequality in capitalist America. Reformist policies such as affirmative action and compensatory education programs, though regarded as ameliorative, are viewed by structuralist theorists as merely providing temporary band-aids to a system that is inherently oppressive:

> The US educational system, in the present nexus of economic power relationships, cannot foster such patterns of personal development and social equality. To reproduce the labor force, the schools are designed to legitimate inequality, limit personal development to forms compatible with submission to arbitrary authority, and aid in the process whereby youth are resigned to their fate. (Bowles and Gintis, 1976, p. 266)

Racism in education is conceptualized as a by-product of the cultural and economic reproduction of a repressed and divided labor force — capitalism does, after all, need a reserve army of labor (Jackubowicz, 1985). However, what is functional for capitalism is, according to structuralists, systematically dysfunctional for humane, egalitarian relationships among different social and cultural groups. Minorities and the working classes are consequently forced to bear the costs of capitalism's uneven development. How, then, are these unequal relationships to be reversed? Bowles and Gintis (1976) argue that nothing short of revolutionary socialist change can guarantee genuine equality for the oppressed:

> A socialist revolution is the shift of control over the process of production from the minority of capitalists, managers and bureaucrats to the producers themselves. The move toward democratic and participatory economic relationships makes possible the breakdown of the hierarchical division of labor and the antagonistic relationships among groups of workers vying for positions in the stratification system (e.g., between blacks and whites, men and women, white and blue-collar workers). It unleashes the possibility of turning technology and organization toward unalienated social relationships. By undermining the social subordination of working people, it allows the emergence of a truly democratic consciousness — both political and economic — of the citizenry. By removing the economic base of class oppression, it permits the construction of social institutions — such as schools — which foster rather than repress the individual's struggle for autonomy and personal development while providing the social framework for making this a truly cooperative struggle. (p. 283)

Structuralists do propose an interim role for education and educators in the process of the transition to socialism. Education is seen as having a critical role to play in developing the kind of democratic consciousness that would help to 'eliminate racial and sexual discrimination' (Bowles and Gintis, 1976, p. 267). The promotion of a democratic consciousness in education would also help to 'liberate a vast pool of relatively untapped talents, abilities, and human resources for productive purposes' (Bowles and Gintis, 1976, p. 268). The role of the teacher/educator in this process is that of a subversive who, on the one hand, works toward democratization of the school process, and on the other, attempts to build organic links with politically active movements in the community (Bowles and Gintis, 1976; Edari, 1984; Sarup, 1986).

Compared to the very specific reforms promoted by mainstream educators, neo-Marxist proposals in the area of race and educational reform are somewhat vague. And race-relations reform is presented within structuralist frameworks as an ancillary matter in a broader project of building a socialist society. It is not clear what role minorities might play either in the current transitional phase of pre-socialism or within the projected new American socialist society itself. It is also worth remarking that structuralists such as Edari (1984) ignore or dismiss out of hand already existing and minority-led efforts for educational change in race relations. Despite their limitations, projects such as multicultural and bilingual education are directly informed by black, Hispanic and Native American struggles over the curriculum. Unfortunately, the issues of identity, representation and meaning raised by these curriculum struggles are accorded secondary importance within structuralist approaches to the struggle against capitalism. This essentially proletarian vision of education and social change also fails to address adequately the issues concerning the nonsynchronous intersection of race, class and gender within the institutional setting of schools. As we saw, earlier, these issues of differential interests, needs and so forth, constitute formidable obstacles to the building of alliances against the status quo and the realization of policy reforms in race relations in education.

The Culturalists

Unlike Marxist structuralists, curriculum theorists who take a culturalist approach to schools are far more inclined to emphasize the pivotal importance of education in current struggles against the status quo. Critical curriculum theorists such as Wood (1985), for instance, accord a greater role than do structuralist educators to teachers, students and the curriculum in the political project of transforming existing race, class and gender relations in school and society. Although, like Marxist structuralist educators, some critical curriculum theorists make a strong case for socialism as the form of society that could best resolve the problem of severe inequality currently experienced by minorities and working classes in capitalist America, they view this objective of socialist transformation as a long-term political project.

This notion of a long-term political project rooted in the daily practices and experiences of subordinated groups is described rather eloquently by Williams (1961) as the 'long revolution'. The concept of the long revolution partly involves a decentered notion of political power and political practice and a recognition that there are already in existence consequential struggles and practical alternatives generated by subaltern groups of teachers, students and workers in their own institutional settings. Some critical curriculum theorists, such as Apple (1982), argue that it is possible for radical educators to consolidate and build upon existing counter-hegemonic initiatives already undertaken by teachers and students within educational institutions:

If we see culture and politics as providing sites of struggles, then counter-hegemonic work within these spheres becomes important. If cultural form and content and the state (as well as the economy) are inherently contradictory, and if these contradictions are lived out in the school itself by students and teachers, then the range of possible actions is expanded considerably. (Apple, 1982, p. 166)

Critical curriculum theorists also maintain that the school is not 'innocent' of contradictions of race, class and gender (Carnoy and Levin, 1985; Connell, *et al.*, 1982; Wood, 1985). They suggest that the role of the teacher should be that of an activist for democratic reforms in the school setting. Teachers should help students to better analyze and struggle against inequalities of power and resources in school and society. Connell *et al.* make the following claim:

Education has fundamental connections with the idea of human emancipation, though it is constantly in danger of being captured for other interests. In a society disfigured by class exploitation, sexual and racial oppression, and in chronic danger of war and environmental destruction, the only education worth the name is one that forms people capable of taking part in their own liberation. The business of school is not propaganda. It is equipping people with the knowledge and skills and concepts relevant to remaking a dangerous and disordered world. In the most basic sense, the process of education and the process of liberation are the same ... At the beginning of the 1980s it is plain that the forces opposed to that growth here and on the world scale are not only powerful but have become increasingly militant. In such circumstances, education becomes a risky enterprise. Teachers too have to decide whose side they are on. (1982, p. 208)

Wood (1985) attempts to make these arguments more concrete by suggesting the rearticulation of current curricular concerns with basic competency in math, reading and science with a more radical notion of 'critical literacy'. By critical literacy, Wood refers to the process of helping students to understand the structures of decision-making in the state and in the economy that effectively work to perpetuate the marginalization of oppressed minorities and working-class men and women. The curriculum, Wood argues, must offer alternatives:

A simple example from our work in Appalachia can illuminate this. While rich in natural resources, the Appalachian region continues to be one of the poorest in the country. One of the main tools used to exploit the region is known as a broad-form deed, clauses of which entitle those holding title to minerals to remove them any way they see fit — including strip mining. Further, many of these mineral rights deeds grossly undervalue the raw materials removed. Utilizing these deeds as a basic element of the curriculum, one can teach reading (vocabulary), math, law, economics, etc., and at the same time open up the ways in which these documents deprive the people of the region of their rich birthright. Additionally, exploring how these documents are able to survive legal challenges without becoming part of a political discourse not only teaches 'subject matter,' but raises questions about the legitimacy of the entire political system. Thus, students become critically literate — not only able 'to read' and 'do math,' but able to penetrate the very structures that oppress them. This is the first step toward a pedagogy for democratic participation. (1985, pp. 106–7)

Marxist culturalist educators and critical curriculum theorists such as Wood have raised several provocative issues concerning education and social change. The notion of building within the school a 'counter-hegemonic pedagogy' and critical civics curriculum directed at presenting American school youth with alternatives 'to the accepted order' (Wood, 1985, p. 108) opens up possibilities within everyday pedagogical practices for the exploration of issues of racial inequality. But critical curriculum theorists, like Marxist structuralists, fall far short of offering clear alternatives that would directly address the issues of race and inequality. These more culturalist school critics also fail to specify programmatic approaches that would really come to grips with the problems associated with the nonsynchronous intersection of race, class and gender in the institutional setting and the fact that competing interests among minorities, women and working-class people can help to undermine alliances among these groups. In the next section of this chapter, I will offer some basic principles of what I wish to call a nonsynchronous approach to race-relations reform that attempts to address some of the knotty issues associated with minority/majority encounters in educational institutions and in society.

Race and Educational Reform: Coming to Terms with Nonsynchrony

> Among many champions of racial equality there is a tendency to see black people as a homogeneous mass and to implicitly assume that they are so different from any other group in society that the standard variables do not apply to them. With the exception that the stereotypes this creates are benign rather than malign, this differs little from the racist approach. (Fitzgerald, 1984, pp. 53–4)

As we have seen, mainstream and radical approaches to race-relations reform do not adequately address the diverse needs and interests of embattled minority groups in the institutional context of schools. These inadequacies in current approaches to race and educational reform hinge on important theoretical as well as strategic questions and are evident in three critical areas.

First, both mainstream and radical theorists have paid little attention to the internal relations of competition and cultural selection within education and to the specific operation of race in the institutional setting — particularly its complex intersection with variables of class and gender. I have argued, for instance, that minority needs and interests are neither homogeneous nor unitary and that the intersection of these raced, classed and gendered interests in the unequal institutional environment of schools is systematically contradictory or nonsynchronous. In short, nonsynchrony directly informs the shape of interests and needs in education and other institutions. As I showed in Chapter 5, race-relations reforms and policy initiatives are likely to

be constrained, or even subverted, if these multiple and often conflicting interests and needs are not properly addressed. Indeed, liberal
and radical failure to take into account the political and programmatic
implications of nonsynchrony is both remarkable and ironic when one
considers the political mileage that the current conservative US administration has gotten out of exploiting exactly these nonsynchronous
differences among minority groups in critical race-relations arenas
and institutions such as the Civil Rights Commission. For instance,
by deploying neo-conservative and self-interested petty bourgeois
minority officials on the boards of racially strategic organizations such
as the Civil Rights Commission, the Reagan and Bush administrations
have been able to call on articulate black support to lead the
ideological defense of some of their most racist and anti-reformist
policies on a wide range of issues — affirmative action, desegregation,
abortion, gay and lesbian rights, and so on.

A second shortcoming of current approaches to race-relations
reform has been that both liberal and radical educators have failed to
theorize and strategize adequately around the state and its uneven and
variable 'involvement' in racial relations between blacks and whites in
education and society in the United States. Thus, while liberal educators have tended (somewhat naively) to regard the state as neutral,
impartial and open to rational arguments, radical theorists have tended
to focus almost exclusively on the state's class character rather than on
its specific racial dimensions. This underestimation of the racial character of the state can be costly, as the fate of a number of educational
reforms introduced or promoted by liberal educators and policy intellectuals has illustrated.

A very good example of the highly racialized and uneven effects
of the state's implementation of educational reform is illustrated in the
case of the state's enforcement of desegregation policy and the impact
this has had on the autonomy of black-controlled institutions. It is
important to remind ourselves that legislation concerning desegregation (Title IV and Title VI of the 1964 Civil Rights Act) was the
culmination of liberal reformist efforts and minority activism for
equality of opportunity. Jim Crow segregationist policies in the South
and institutional racism in the North effectively constrained minority
youth to inferior education in poorly funded schools and colleges.
The ostensible policy intention behind desegregation guidelines was to
equalize the educational experiences of minority and majority youth
through the expedient of racial integration of blacks into white-
dominated institutions and vice versa. But the state's procedural
implementation of this desegregation policy has had a powerful

discriminatory effect on black-majority educational institutions. While the enforcement of desegregation guidelines has almost never meant that white Americans have been in danger of losing control and autonomy over white-dominated institutions, the same has not been true for historically black-dominated institutions. Marable (1985) makes this clear by giving some examples:

> Title IV of the 1964 Civil Rights Act forced Black public institutions to merge with neighboring all-white schools. By the early 1980s, Lincoln University of Missouri and the University of Maryland–Eastern Shore, both historically Black institutions, had majority-white student bodies ... Federal courts did little or nothing about the continuation of segregation at white universities, while pressuring Black colleges to conform to desegregation guidelines. On 20 July 1984, for example, one US district judge declared that Tennessee State University could no longer be allowed to keep its 'Black identity.' Any retention of a predominantly Black faculty and a Black president was a 'situation which has got to change.' (Marable, 1985, p. 102)

This brings us to the third area in which current approaches to race-relations reform are somewhat underdeveloped. Both mainstream and radical educators have failed to explore genuinely or to engage with the rich history of struggle, experiences and points of view that have been generated within minority communities and among other politically active groups in the society. Johnson (quoted in Wood, 1985) draws attention to the fact that activist educators must expand the sphere of relevant political action over educational reform by engaging in genuine dialogue with already constituted 'interest' groups:

> Being actively educative is not just a question of 'carrying a policy to the public' or destroying myths about public education. It involves really listening to popular experiences of formal education. It involves research centering around particular struggles and local issues. It involves making links with other agencies — researchers, community activists, black groups, women's groups — not to take them over, but to learn from their experiences and practices. (Johnson, quoted in Wood, 1985, p. 101)

Whether considered individually or collectively, these limitations in current approaches to race-relations reform point to the nonsynchronous relationship that exists between educational reformers and oppressed minority groups. They underscore 'real' differences of interests that in turn militate against a sense of common purpose between reformist educators and intellectuals and the socially disadvantaged. However, as was the case with respect to the more theoretical aspects of the race-education couplet, mainstream and radical silences on issues of institutional complexity, the role of the state and the role of minority groups in the radical movement for educational reform are instructive. It is in part these provocative silences that can help to motivate the formulation of alternative propositions on race relations and education change.

Let me elaborate. Contemporary educators have tended to talk past each other on the subject of racial inequality and the need for educational reform. For example, mainstream educational reformers have tended to concentrate on the microlevel aspects of race relations, focusing on issues of minority academic achievement, teacher expectations and curriculum content. Radical educators have directed their efforts at issues of macrostructural transformation, paying special attention to the economy, the labor process and, to a lesser extent, the state. Attempts to theorize and strategize around the microlevel politics of institutional inequality and their interconnections with struggles at the macrolevel of the economy have been partial at best (Marxist cultural critics and critical curriculum theorists being something of an exception). I believe that an interactive approach to race-relations reform is warranted — one that, for example, attempts to link concerns with such issues as individual achievement and minority representation in the curriculum to a concern over jobs, immigration policies and child care for minority working mothers.

I have maintained throughout that the multifaceted nature of race and its operation in education and society requires a many-sided response — one that recognizes that minorities are not simply oppressed as racial subjects, but are positioned as classed and gendered subjects as well. These dynamics of race, class and gender are interwoven, in an uneven manner, into the social fabric of the institutions and structures of American society — in the educational system, the economy and the state. This uneven interaction of race with other variables, namely class and gender — a process that I have called nonsynchrony — is a practical matter that defines the daily encounter of minority and majority actors in institutional and social settings.

Thus, the experience of educational inequality for a black middle-class male youth is qualitatively different from that of a black working-class girl from a female-headed household. For example, as we saw in the case of Spring's (1985) report on Black Suburbia in Chapter 5, black middle-class youth had more material options than their working-class peers when the racially motivated inferior education in Black Suburbia's public schools became intolerable. The parents of these middle-class youth pulled them out of the public school system and placed them in private educational institutions. Black working-class youth did not have this maneuverability — their parents could not afford to pull them out of the racist public school system.

These issues of nonsynchrony shape and structure the experience of inequality and the micro- and macrodynamics of educational and social life. Nonsynchrony must be factored into any broad-ranged strategy for an alternative approach to race-relations reform. What, then, are the elements of a nonsynchronous interactive approach to race and educational reform? How should we begin to mount an offensive against the educational and social disadvantages that marginalize differentiated minority groups? I would like to use the remainder of this final chapter to paint in rather broad brushstrokes the principal elements of this alternative approach to race-relations reform.

To begin with, I wish to acknowledge that we are in a specific historical conjuncture in the evolution of race relations in the United States — one in which racial antagonism and evidence of increasing minority disadvantage in education and the economy are prominent features of social life (Crichlow, 1990; *Education Week*, 14 May 1986; Marable, 1985; Omi and Winant, 1986; Viadero, 1989). We must, however, resist facile solutions to these issues. Even more critically, we must avoid the temptation to respond to the problem of racial inequality in an undifferentiated and essentialist manner. An essentialist approach to race typically ignores or flattens out the differences within minority groups while at the same time insulating the problem of racial inequality from issues of class and sexual oppression. In the past, while such reformist approaches to racial inequality have benefited a small, upwardly mobile element of the minority population, significant sections of the minority community (particularly inner-city youth and lower-class minority women) have been bypassed.

However, an emergent theory and practice of nonsynchrony must not merely be negative in its implications. It is not enough to critique existing theoretical and programmatic approaches to race and educational reform. The articulation of a nonsynchronous perspective entails a second, more positive conceptual and practical task — that is to stake out a field within contemporary debates on schooling for a more inclusive, affirmative politics that takes seriously the differential needs, interests and desires of minority men and women and urban working-class youth. This positive theoretical and practical intervention in current educational debates involves the affirmation of alternative political, cultural and ideological practices that help to define the identity and efficacy of subordinated groups.

For example, it is important to assert that even the very cultural differences in language, history and subjectivity which dominant educators have diagnosed as minorities' 'symptoms of inadequacy' (JanMohamed and Lloyd, 1987, p. 10) are capable of being re-read transformatively as constituting alternative practices radically opposed to the dominant culture. Indeed, it is precisely these marginalized themes of minority agency, language and cultural identity that black feminist writers such as Zora Neale Hurston (1978), June Jordan (1980) and Ntozake Shange (1983) have mobilized into a powerful insurgent discourse that challenges current stereotypical representation of minority people reproduced in dominant American literature and popular culture (McCarthy and Apple, 1988). And it is also these issues of cultural identity, language and difference that have historically defined minority struggles in education for community control and alternative schooling.

Of course, in affirming the positive moment in minority history and struggles in the US, a nonsynchronous perspective should not fall back on the idea of race as some essentialist expression of language and cultural solidarity. Neither should we rush headlong into the politics of cultural exceptionalism or 'the celebration of cultural diversity for its own sake' (JanMohamed and Lloyd, 1987, p. 10). Rather, racial difference must be seen as one of a variety of starting points for drawing out the various solidarities among subordinated minorities, women and working-class youth over our separate but related forms of oppression. In this way, we also move beyond tendencies to treat 'race' as a stable, measurable deposit or category. Racial difference is, therefore, to be understood as a subject-position that can only be properly defined in 'political terms' (JanMohamed and Lloyd, 1987) — that is, in terms of the effects of struggles over social and economic exploitation, political disenfranchisement and cultural and ideological repression. In this respect, discourses over education and racial inequality cannot be meaningfully separated from discourses over issues such as police brutality in black neighborhoods or the sexual and mental harassment of minority women on the shop floor (Carby, 1982; Hicks, 1981; Parmar, 1982). We also come to recognize that examining race relations is critical, not simply for an understanding of social life as it exists in the margins of American society, but ultimately for an understanding of life as it is expressed in the broad political and economic mainstream of this country. For as Hall (1981) maintains:

> If you try to stop the story about racial politics, racial divi-
> sions, racist ideologies short of confronting some of these
> difficult issues; if you present an idealized picture of a 'multi-
> cultural' or 'ethnically varied' society which doesn't look at the
> way in which racism has acted back inside the working class
> itself, the way in which racism has combined with, for exam-
> ple, sexism working back within the black population itself; if
> you try to tell the story as if somewhere around the corner
> some whole constituted class is waiting for a green light to
> advance and displace the racist enemy . . . you will have done
> absolutely nothing whatsoever for the political understanding
> of your students. (p. 68)

It is this recognition of the interrelated and overdetermined nature of race relations in schooling and society that helps to define the
principal task ahead: to reconstruct current mainstream and radical
approaches to race and educational reform which now focus either too
narrowly on classroom practices or too abstractly on capital-labor
relations in the workplace. The nonsynchronous approach to race-
relations reform therefore follows a different path and proceeds in a
non-dogmatic manner to link initiatives for race-relations reform in
education to wider struggles for change in existing class and patriarchal relations in capitalist society. Minorities, as I have pointed out,
are already positioned in these multiple struggles as raced, classed
and gendered subjects. In a related sense, also, the nonsynchronous
approach deliberately avoids the privileging of particular sites of
struggle such as the trade union, the political party or the state.
Instead, I argue for a strategic Marxism — or what Apple (1979, 1982,
1986) calls a politics of 'non-reformist reforms' — that attempts to
build 'integrated' political projects and alliances from within the
already constituted hegemonic struggles and everyday practices of
teachers, students, parents, administrators and minority and working-
class youth. This broad-based interactive approach to race-relations
reform can be subdivided into three interrelated spheres of strategic
action, namely, state/society initiatives, institutional initiatives in

education (schools, colleges, universities and so forth) and curriculum and pedagogical initiatives in the classroom.

State/Society initiatives: Setting the agenda

It is customary in mainstream and radical literature on race and educational reform to discuss the state as if 'it' were a central and coherent organization or edifice that resided outside society itself. Mainstream educators tend to regard the state as an impartial actor, an enforcer of laws, the ultimate recourse for resolution of racial (and other 'political') matters. On the other hand, radical educators operate from a tradition that regards the state as 'interventionist' — acting to stabilize popular demands in society and to facilitate capitalist accumulation and super-exploitation of racially subordinated labor (Bowles and Gintis, 1976; Edari, 1984). Recent research on race and the state has begun to point in new and important directions that are helpful for thinking about race-relations reform. Drawing primarily on the work of the Italian Marxist Gramsci, writers such as Hall (1988) and Troyna and Williams (1986) have begun to break down the state/mass dichotomy that is so often invoked in the research literature on the state. Instead, these writers insist on the idea of an 'extended' or 'integrated' state deeply invaded by the popular organizations of civil society. For instance, Ben–Tovim, Gabriel, Law and Stredder (1982) contend that the integrated state comprises:

> both formal institutions, made up principally of central and local governments and their administrative apparatuses, and informal or private institutions, including those representing industrial and financial sectors of the economy, trade unions, political parties, voluntary organizations and so on. (p. 307)

This notion of an integrated or extended state draws attention to the state as a site for the production of nonsynchronous racial politics (Burawoy, 1981). In the US, popular sensibility around this expanded notion of the state and the public sphere was dramatically realized in the anti-racist, anti-establishment and anti-war politics of the 1960s and early 1970s. The literal invasion of the state by 'popular' demands for racial justice in housing, education and employment helped to set the political priorities for state action in a variety of spheres. But even with this expanded context, racial politics during this period remained paradigmatically insulated from discourses over working-class and gender struggles — a factor that was firmly crystallized in some of the sexist features of the internal organization and public rhetoric of the civil rights movement and black nationalist groups. (Of course, this observation does not in any way subtract from the fact that the civil rights movement did play a generative role in broad protest movements emerging in the 1960s: both the feminist movement and anti-war movement drew inspiration and strategy from the civil rights movement.)

Given the lessons learned from the past, progressive and radical groups must work toward regaining a moral offensive within the state over racial inequality in education. But in the 1990s and beyond, this must mean the democratization of the internal politics of reformist movements themselves. Radical educators must struggle *with* and not *for* the socially disadvantaged; minority men must engage with the problems of minority women; and working-class organizations must struggle with the problems of racism and sexism. Racial inequality in education cannot be separated from this broad range of issues. It must be remembered that inequality in education for black youth has historically been associated with inequality of opportunity and unequal futures in virtually all other spheres of social, economic and political life. In this sense, then, challenges to racial inequality and the inferior quality of educational experiences that minority youth endure will be futile if these challenges are not connected to a generalized offensive maintained within and outside the state with respect to issues such as unemployment, health care and police harassment. These issues of minority disadvantage intersect (however unevenly) with similar, if not identical, issues of deprivation faced by working-class male and female youth. Of course, we should not be too hasty in our assumptions of common ground among the differentially oppressed. The task of building alliances around issues of educational inequality and social deprivation will involve trade-offs, compromises and so forth. But the task of building a sense of purpose, political will and moral leadership within an integrated state (among 'progressive' and reformist administrative officials, legislators, teachers, students and minority and women's groups) over issues of inequality — racism, sexism, class oppression — must not be abandoned.

These goals must be pursued in the context of establishing a new social agenda and redefining priorities for state policies and programs that can help make a difference in the lives of minorities and other oppressed groups. This process of agenda-setting is crucial in that it summarizes the state's relationship to civil society and defines the direction and focus of the state's political and moral leadership over the plurality of social, economic and cultural issues of our time. Just as critically, the process of agenda-setting also clarifies where and to what ends technical, political and economic resources harnessed in the public sector will be expended and who will be the beneficiaries (capitalist enterprise, the military, minority and women's groups, the unemployed, etc.) of state policies and programs. This process should not be taken for granted and the political participation or non-participation of popular organizations is crucial in determining what will become the principal preoccupations of the state.

I believe that radical educators can ill afford to stand outside the 'conventional' politics of policy formulation. To do so is, in fact, to forfeit considerable political ground to conservative and mainstream actors positioned in state institutions and apparatuses. By remaining outside the processes of policy-making and agenda-setting, radical actors also avoid the very difficult task of generating options and alternatives that would address the everyday needs and interests of oppressed minorities and women. In significant ways, radical educators have already conceded considerable ground and leverage to mainstream educators in the determination of education and social policy. This has been powerfully illustrated in the unfolding of political events in the last decade in the United States.

In a time of conservative restoration, the state has redirected funds and resources away from the policy commitments to assuaging minority disadvantage in education and society that were established under more liberal administrations in the 1960s. With the ascendancy of the Reagan administration in the 1980s, commitments to expanding the United States military and defense capability and aggressive policies of privatization and deregulation supplanted concerns with poverty and inequality that had been critical features of earlier liberal policy agendas. These developments have been particularly felt in the area of race relations and education. For example, the state has drastically scaled down its monetary commitment to compensatory and remedial education programs that have principally ministered to the needs of minority and working-class youth. Indeed, as Bastian, Fruchter, Gittell, Greer and Haskins (1986) have pointed out, 'disadvantaged students with basic skills needs are receiving significantly less remedial help than they received over the past two decades' (p. 83). According to these authors, 'as many as 900,000 students lost Title I services [and some] thirteen states have entirely eliminated specific Title I/Chapter I programs, including math and pre-school programs' (p. 83). With the exception of popular programs like Head Start, this pattern of parsimony and insensitivity to the social and

Figure 6.1   Trends in state policy toward higher education

Higher Education

1960s	Versus	1980s
1 In 1964, the Economic Opportunity Act authorized funding of college work-study programs to assist academically disadvantaged students.		1 In 1980, incoming President Reagan declared his hostility to the federal government's involvement in education and suggested that the Department of Education be abolished.
2 In 1964, the Civil Rights Act was passed prohibiting funding to institutions that discriminated on the basis of race, thereby mandating that colleges and universities open their doors to minorities.		2 In 1983, the Republican administration provided tax exemptions to private institutions — like Bob Jones University — that practiced discrimination and elitism.
3 Under the Higher Education Act of 1965, work-study programs were expanded, a program of need-based grants was established, and federal assistance to struggling black colleges was provided.		3 In its first four years, the Reagan administration used the material and legal resources of the Department of Justice to challenge affirmative action quotas.
4 In 1968, the trio of outreach and academic support programs (Upward Bound, Talent Search and Special Services for Disadvantaged Students) were created.		4 In 1988, the severity of cutbacks initiated by the federal government was felt, particularly in the area of college work-study programs on which many minority students depend for supplementary income while they are in college. Funding for these work-study programs declined by 22 per cent during the period.

educational needs of the disadvantaged has not really changed with George Bush's assumption of office. The 'new' Republican adminis-tration continues to 'stay the [old] course' with respect to its sense of spending priorities, even in the light of the changes that the recent wave of reforms in Europe have brought about regarding the 'military threat from the Soviet bloc'.

These developments are symptomatic of the effective depriori-tization of minority interests and the steady racialization of the state's social and political agenda as formulated by the conservative US administration. This has been the case in areas of special importance to racial minorities such as higher education. Figure 6.1 illustrates and summarizes patterns in state policies with respect to higher education for minority and working-class youth. State policies of the 1960s are compared with the 1980s.

It is vitally important that radical educators directly challenge current patterns of resource allocation in higher education by in-tervening in the process of agenda-setting and policy formulation both at the local level of school board, municipal and state politics and at the national level of federal decision-making. A first task must be to contest the racialization of state policies and the deprioritization of minority interests in the practices of social and economic planning conducted within the state. This is not a matter that can be postponed or treated simply as a 'minority issue,' for underfunding of Title I programs and other social welfare projects also affects working-class youth and women. The heterogeneous organizational, material and intellectual resources of progressive groups must be mobilized in a systematic challenge to the state's discriminatory social policies. Of course, this opens up questions about what types of fiscal policies and expenditures should have priority in the state's agenda. Using the ideologically charged discourse of 'national interest' and 'national security', policy-makers have sought to justify excessive state allocations to defense (even in the present post-Cold War times) and the corresponding underfunding of ameliorative educational projects such as compensatory education. In the past, radical educators and social activists have too easily conceded to mainstream intellectuals and policy-makers the definition of what ought to constitute the 'national interest'. By drawing attention to the state's responsibility to its least endowed citizenry — minority and working-class men and women — radical educators and activists can help to redefine the discourse of 'national interest' in a manner that would include the needs and interests of these oppressed groups.

Second, radical educators and activists must work towards containing efforts to erode the ameliorative gains made by and through the struggles of minorities and women in education and employment — gains that have come under vicious attacks by conservative policy-makers in recent years. As Bastian *et al.* (1986) have argued, specific ameliorative programs such as bilingual education and Head Start, which have helped to enhance minority educational and material improvement, must be defended. But it is necessary to go beyond a mere stabilization of minority and working-class gains in education derived from the struggles and compromises of a previous decade. Radical educators must be willing to go one step further and argue for an expanded and radically egalitarian program of reforms that would link minority demands for equality in education to demands for structural and economic changes in US urban centers. Such broad-based egalitarian reforms would help to support and enhance the quality of life for oppressed minorities and working-class women and men. This would mean the development of infrastructural supports for job creation, health care, child care, decent housing and community autonomy and control of social services, including education. In other words, reforms that attempt to enhance minority school success must be 'integrated' into a more comprehensive framework of policies aimed at the restoration and development of minority and working-class communities in the inner city as well as fostering the economic, cultural and political participation of minorities and working-class women and men in the social life of this country.

The political project of redirecting the state's agenda away from the hegemony of mainstream conservative policy discourses and toward the non-paradigmatic inclusion of the nonsynchronous needs, interests and demands of differentially oppressed groups lays the basis for a genuine democratization of contemporary policy frameworks and an expansion of the 'public's' access to the resources harnessed in the state. This process of democratization and redefinition of the state's policy agenda should also help to set the stage for policy reform in race relations at the institutional level of schools, colleges and universities.

Institutional Initiatives: Working Toward a Genuinely Egalitarian School Culture

The internal dynamics of educational institutions such as schools are particularly complex and often unstable. This complexity is shaped by the plurality of actors and interests that literally clash with and mutually subvert each other within the school environment. Mainstream reformist discourses have tended to ignore the issues of the intersection of race, class and gender and the internal 'rules' or relations of competition, exploitation, domination and cultural selection which mediate social and cultural differences in the school. Let me be more specific. Significant and, in some cases, vast differences in assets, capacities, interests and needs separate minority students from majority students and minority teachers from majority teachers in schools. For example, the simple factor of numerical difference in representation and presence on school faculties and school boards at white-dominated institutions almost always translates into enormous racial imbalances in power and influence within the decision-making processes in education. For minority teachers and students, being outnumbered often means being outorganized and outmaneuvered (Small-McCarthy, 1988).

But the matter goes further than numbers. The formal and informal institutional rules of competition, exploitation, domination and cultural selection in schools operate to the benefit of dominant whites and to the disadvantage of minorities. Troyna and Williams (1986), for example, argue that black students and black teachers are particularly vulnerable to the sociocultural rules of educational institutions — rules that are often refereed by their white peers. ('Blacks are almost always compelled to become "cultural experts" on terms which are dictated by white professionals', Troyna and Williams, 1986, p. 118.) These race-relations theorists offer a concrete example of this institutional dilemma for minorities in the British educational context by drawing attention to 'the controversy in Birmingham in 1985 over a special management course for black teachers, on the grounds that they were under-performing professionally' (Troyna and Williams, 1986, p. 118).

Given the fact that the highly differentiated educational system benefits whites relative to their minority colleagues, why should white teachers and administrators be interested in race-relations reform? Mainstream educational reformers have for too long operated on a model of the school as a culturally neutral institution. This depoliticized approach to reform also limits the problem of racial inequality in American schooling to the seemingly manageable, but simplistically construed, issue of 'black underachievement'. Typically, policy reformers ignore the needs and interests of teachers and students and the micropolitics associated with the endogenous institutional differences that shape minority/majority relations in schooling.

Mainstream and radical educators also fail to explore the gendered nature of teachers' work and the way in which practical constraints and impediments in the daily lives and experiences of teachers can militate against the implementation or realization of educational reforms. For instance, increased rationalization of educational institutions has meant that the working environments of many schools are often 'restrictive, impersonal, organizationally rigid, understaffed' (Bastian, *et al.*, 1986, p. 25). In addition, considerable evidence now exists that shows that even at the most elite of American schools, most teachers are overworked, underpaid and increasingly stripped of autonomy over critical dimensions of their work, such as the determination of curriculum content, course materials and discipline (Goodlad, 1983; Sizer, 1984). These structuring features of the daily institutional and working culture of teachers must be taken into account in any proposals for race-relations reform in schooling. It is, in my view, absolutely critical that educational reformers refrain from the current practice of treating schools as empty boxes into and onto which one merely dumps reformist policies from the outside. It is this highly decontextualized approach to schooling that has imperiled many well-intended mainstream reforms. Reformist policy initiatives such as public school desegregation have often meant simply increasing the numbers and visibility of minorities in student and faculty bodies of the schools. Educators and policy-makers have by and large failed to address the organizational and institutional cultures of schools and the ways in which related institutional practices delimit minority/ majority choices and options for or against educational change.

Above all, it is important to point out that reform in race relations in education must be worked for and struggled over if change is to be meaningfully incorporated into the daily lives of teachers and students. This means working for a fundamental institutional commitment to rethinking current curriculum and educational priorities. It means, for example, rethinking the educational emphasis that is currently being placed on 'excellence' and 'efficiency' at the expense of concerns over equity. But even more crucially, race-relations reform must engage with the nonsynchronous rules of competition, exploitation, domination and cultural selection — the fundamental institutional rules of the game that mediate social class, gender and race differences in the school environment. We must strive to achieve a new set of priorities in the institutional environment of the school — priorities that emphasize cultural inclusion instead of cultural selection, cooperation over competition, democratization and equity over domination and exploitation.

Some of the elements necessary for this reprioritization and reorganization are already present as countervailing features of the school environment. There is, as Carnoy and Levin (1985) have pointed out, a tradition of democratic and ethical values and a language of reciprocity operating within the formal and informal culture of teachers and students in schools. These democratic and ethical elements are often overwhelmed by an instrumental logic and a preoccupation with rationalization and efficiency. It is therefore necessary to resuscitate, consolidate and expand these more democratic and possibilitarian aspects of schooling in order to build a genuinely egalitarian, anti-racist and anti-sexist environment in educational institutions. In practical terms, this may mean certain forms of so-called 'positive discrimination' to 'correct' a history of educational marginalization and neglect of minority students. For example, nonsynchronous emancipatory institutional initiatives might involve the principle that 'underachieving' minority students are given first priority with respect to access to resources, teacher time and so forth, based on the Rawlsian principle of 'maximizing the advantage of the least advantaged' (Apple, 1979, p. 32). A process of reprioritization in schooling based on the principles I have suggested — along with a process of reprioritization in the state/society agenda on race and educational reform — would facilitate the development and fostering of a genuinely egalitarian institutional culture that, if anything, would privilege the needs of the least rather than the most advantaged among us.

Curriculum Initiatives

Reformist initiatives to foster egalitarian social relations in the school environment also foreground the need for a more democratic and egalitarian approach to curriculum and pedagogical practices in education. In this matter, certain facts have become painfully clear. There is now considerable documentation in both mainstream and radical literature indicating stagnation and, in some cases, reversals in the educational fortunes of black, Hispanic and Native American youth as we enter decade of the 1990s (Gamoran and Berends, 1986; Grant, 1984, 1985; Sudarkasa, 1988). These studies also draw attention to some of the most pernicious ways in which current curriculum and pedagogical practices militate against minority success and alienate minority students from an academic core curriculum. For instance, studies show the following: that minority girls and boys are more likely than their white peers to be placed in low or non-academic tracks (Fordham, 1990; Grant, 1984, 1985); that teachers' encouragement and expectations of academic performance are considerably lower for black and Hispanic students than for white students (Ogbu and Matute-Bianchi, 1986); that black students have access to fewer instructional opportunities than white students (Gamoran and Berends, 1986); and that ultimately, black, Hispanic and Native American youth are more likely to drop out of school than white youth (*Education Week*, 14 May 1986; Swartz, 1989). These racial factors are complicated by dynamics of gender (black girls fare better academically than black boys but are more likely to be denied the academic and social status accorded to white girls and white boys in the classroom, Grant, 1984, 1985; Ogbu, 1978) and dynamics of class (increasingly, black PMC youth are abandoning predominantly black institutions and opting for white-dominated state colleges and Ivy League universities, thereby imperiling the autonomy and the survival of black institutions and raising disturbing questions about cultural identity, Marable, 1985).

As we have seen, mainstream responses to the problem of race and education have tended to stress the social liabilities of minorities and to promote compensatory curriculum and educational programs of the following kinds:

a)   cultural and educational enrichment programs such as Head Start and Upward Bound;
b)   multicultural curricula that place emphasis on building minority self-concept and self-esteem;
c)   back-to-basics and competencies-oriented programs aimed at equipping minority youth for the secondary labor market.

The usefulness of individual programs such as Head Start notwith-standing, mainstream educators have tended to paste over the central contradictions associated with race and the curriculum and have attempted instead to impose an instrumental regime on curriculum and pedagogical practices in education. These approaches to curricu-lum and educational reform have consequently had the effect of stabi-lizing rather than challenging the *modus operandi* of schooling and the curriculum practices of ability-grouping and tracking — the principal mechanisms through which minorities are culturally excluded from an academic core curriculum and 'prepared' for the secondary labor mar-ket. These practices of curriculum differentiation — the teaching of different types of curricula to different groups of students — also constitute the core processes of racial marginalization and subordina-tion of minority students in the institutional culture of the school.

In fundamental ways, then, mainstream educators and policy intellectuals have failed to engage teachers in a sustained examination of the sociological and racial dimensions of current curriculum and pedagogical practices. The issue of race and equity in education re-quires a serious rethinking of current curriculum and pedagogical practices of tracking and ability-grouping (Bastian *et al.*, 1986; Crich-low, 1990). All students should have access to an academic 'core' curriculum. The fact that disproportionate numbers of America's black, Hispanic and Native American youth are now alienated from such a curriculum in the public schools is both intolerable and inde-fensible.

But the idea of a general academic core curriculum also poses direct questions about the content and organization of materials with-in the school curriculum. For instance, continued Anglocentric domi-nance in the content and organization of American school curricula underscores the fact that educators have merely paid lip service to minority demands for greater inclusion of knowledge about the his-tory and culture of Hispanics, blacks and Native Americans. Even the relatively modest proposals of multicultural education proponents have not been taken seriously in most programs (Banks, 1981, 1987).

Nevertheless, as school populations become more ethnically diverse, and minorities become the majorities in many school districts across the country, the moral and practical support for the hegemony of Anglocentrism in the curriculum has been imperiled (Schmidt, 1989). The hegemonic truce that has existed over the years between school authorities and the rapidly diversifying constituencies which they serve has become frayed. Minority youth and women have begun to challenge the assumptions and practices that undergird the selection of school knowledge and the content of college and university curricula. Questions are being raised about 'traditional dichotomies such as the division between the hard "masculine" subjects like mathematics and the sciences, and the soft "feminine" arts subjects' (Sarup, 1986, p. 117). Minority students are once again mounting 'new' demands for democratization and diversity in the curriculum and course offerings of schools and universities across the country. It is at this point of rupture within the dominant curriculum paradigm that more radical demands for critical anti-racist and anti-sexist curricular materials and pedagogical practices can be introduced. As radical critics such as Connell (1987) and Sarup (1986) have argued, the school curriculum for minority and majority youth should have an organic link to other experiences and struggles within the society, with respect to such issues as the policing of minority neighborhoods, sexual harassment and marginalization of minority and majority women in the workplace, and the infrastructural needs of minority communities in America's urban centers and inner cities. Such a 'new' critical curriculum would also 'celebrate the contributions of working people, women, and minorities to our general cultural pool' and would be the point of departure 'for providing students with their own cultural capital' (Wood, 1985, p. 107). By insisting on the introduction into the school curriculum of radically diverse cultural knowledge(s) rooted in the social bases and nonsynchronous experiences of oppressed groups, we can move beyond the 'benign' pluralism and cultural relativism of mainstream programs as embodied in certain innocuous forms of multicultural education. For as Abdul JanMohamed and David Lloyd (1987) argue, 'Such pluralism tolerates the existence of salsa, it even enjoys Mexican restaurants, but it bans Spanish as a medium of instruction in American schools' (p. 10).

But merely moving beyond simplistic models of cultural relativism is not enough to 'invert the hegemony' (Connell, 1987, p. 15) of dominant Anglocentrism in the curriculum. We must go further than the compensatory strategy of simply adding diverse cultural knowledge(s) onto the dominant curriculum. A nonsynchronous approach to the transformation of school knowledge requires a second strategy, one aimed at promoting nonsynchrony, difference and heterogeneity as what Bob Connell (1987) calls a program of 'common learnings'. Such a strategy aims at reconstructing the dominant curriculum — which we now know legitimates the experiences and practices of the white middle class — by bringing the uninstitutionalized experiences of marginalized minorities and working-class women and men 'to the center' of the organization and arrangement of the school curriculum. The ultimate objective of a 'common learnings' strategy is to seek the generalized diffusion throughout the whole system of schooling of counter-hegemonic knowledge based on the experiences of the disadvantaged. Connell argues for such a pro-active and generative approach to 'universalizing' the nonsynchronous experiences and perspectives of oppressed groups in the curriculum.

Connell's argument rests on two important principles. First, he suggests that a political and ethical principle of positive social justice should inform the selection of knowledge in the school curriculum. In advancing the notion of an expanded approach to educational and social justice, Connell also suggests that a 'new' critical curriculum should privilege the human interests of the least advantaged. Second, he maintains that the nonsynchronous transformation of the school curriculum should be based on epistemological principles that affirm the validity of the points of view of marginalized minorities and working-class men and women. It is useful to quote him in some detail here:

> In principle there are many possible common learnings programs, though in a particular historical setting only a few are likely to be of great practical importance. A minimal criterion for choice among them, and a minimal defence of the strategy of inverting hegemony, is the criterion of social justice. We can accept with Rawls that social justice means taking the standpoint of the least advantaged, though we can do without his fantasy that this might occur in ignorance of one's social position ... But this is only a minimal defence. There are stronger reasons for seeking an educational program constructed in this way. Different standpoints yield different views of the world and some are more comprehensive and powerful than others ... If you wish to teach about ethnicity and race relations, for instance, a more comprehensive and deeper understanding is possible if you construct your curriculum from the point of view of the subordinated ethnic groups than if you work from the point of view of the dominant one.

'Racism' is a qualitatively *better* organizing concept than 'natural inferiority,' though each has it roots in a particular experience and embodies a social interest. [Another] case is provided by the growth of knowledge about gender. There has long been a body of information and discourse about the family, women's employment, children's social development, masculinity and femininity, which remained for decades a backwater in social sciences hegemonised by the interests of men. The standpoint of the least advantaged in gender relations, articulated in feminism, has transformed that. Modern feminism has produced a *qualitatively better* analysis of a large domain of social life through a range of new concepts (sexual politics, patriarchy, the sexual division of labor, etc.) and new research informed by them. The implications of this conceptual revolution are still to be felt across much of the curriculum. (Connell, 1987, pp. 16–18)

Connell's arguments for reconstructing the curriculum from the standpoint of those 'carrying the burdens of social inequality' (p. 17) are well founded. It is true that 'the marginalized, or the oppressed are the only ones who can understand the full significance of oppression' (Edgerton, 1989, p. 3). A critical curriculum, which emphasizes anti-racist and anti-sexist change and social reorganization and utilizes the points of view and experiences of oppressed minorities and working-class women and men as the primary bases for a core curriculum, would constitute a fundamental step in the direction of preparing students for democratic participation in a complex, differential and nonsynchronous world. Of course, we must be ever mindful of the dangers that Freire pointed us to in his volume, *Pedagogy of the Oppressed* — that is, that the oppressed 'are at one and the same time themselves and the oppressor whose consciousness they have internalized' (1970, p. 32). There are no simple guarantees in political or educational life and radical educators must avoid the tendency to reify the oppressed through an activism shrouded in 'monologues, slogans, and communiques' (p. 52). Changes in the curriculum to address the present and the future of race relations in the United States must therefore be founded in dialogue and the recognition that the production of knowledge is systematically relational and heterogeneous.

Ultimately, though, the project of constructing an egalitarian curriculum is integrally related to the other projects that I have already outlined in this chapter, namely, institutional and organizational initiatives for a more egalitarian educational environment and mobilization for reprioritization within the state over issues of race and social and economic change in urban America. These three initiatives constitute the essential elements of a strategic and nonsynchronous politics of race-relations reform that attempts to link the micropolitical and institutional realities of school to the macropolitical imperatives associated with an integrated and expanded state. Such a strategic approach to race relations directly connects issues of race with issues of class and gender.

I also strive to avoid the precarious politics of dogmatism and class and race essentialism — a politics rooted in privileged sites of struggle, such as the workplace or minority culture or language pure and simple. Instead, the nonsynchronous approach to race-relations reform seeks to privilege the principle of building alliances across different interests and different groups of activist educators, oppressed minorities, working-class women and men, and teachers and students. Within this framework, I have argued that the differential curriculum practices and institutional relations that obtain between minorities and whites in education are sites of struggle over inequality — as crucial in their political importance as are the job market, the labor process or the state.

Conclusion

In Chapter 1, I alluded to the social and economic crises that have steadily engulfed US minority communities as we enter the last decade of the twentieth century. A central flash point of these difficulties has been education. Racial minorities, particularly blacks, Hispanics and Native Americans, have not fared well in American schools. In addition to harsh statistics indicating profound racial differences in achievement scores, dropout rates and so forth, minorities also face problems of severe marginalization and alienation from an academic core curriculum.

In *Race and Curriculum*, I have tried to come to grips with these very difficult and seemingly intractable problems of racial inequality in education and society. I have argued that current debates within the educational literature on the theoretical status of racial inequality have been heavily burdened by essentialism and dogmatism. As we have seen, mainstream educators reduce the problem of racial inequality to the issues of underachievement and minority social and cultural deficits — in some ways blaming minorities themselves for the problems associated with race and social disadvantage. Neo-Marxist educators, on the other hand, have tended to subordinate racial inequality to what they see as the more general problem of class oppression, thereby suppressing the importance of race in the project of social emancipation.

In making the case for an alternative way of thinking about racial inequality — what I have called a nonsynchronous approach to race and education — I have argued against essentialism and against current tendencies in reformist curriculum and educational discourses to treat minorities as homogeneous or undifferentiated groups. In contrast, I have sought throughout to draw attention to the vital links that exist between race and the variables of class and gender and to the nonsynchronous or contradictory interests, needs and desires that directly inform minority encounters with majority whites in school and society and profoundly influence the viability and outcome of policies and programs aimed at ameliorating racial disadvantages in education. By drawing attention to nonsynchrony and difference, I have sought to argue for the politicization and democratization of theories on and strategies directed at race-relations reform in a way that involves minorities, women, teachers, students and administrators in a broad-based offensive against inequality in education and society. I believe that such a democratic, broad-based offensive is crucial if the myriad problems associated with racial inequality are to be meaningfully addressed.

References

ADORNO, T.W., FRENKEL-BRUNSWIK, E., LEVINSON, D.J. and SANFORD, R.N. (1950) *The Authoritarian Personality*, New York, Harper.

ALL LONDON TEACHERS AGAINST RACISM AND FASCISM (1984) *Challenging Racism*, London, ALTARF.

ALLIANCE AGAINST WOMEN'S OPPRESSION (1983) 'Poverty not for women only: A critique of the feminization of poverty', *AAWO Discussion Paper 3*, pp. 1–8.

ALLPORT, G. (1954) *The Nature of Prejudice*, New York, Anchor.

ALTHUSSER, L. (1971) 'Ideology and ideological state apparatuses', in *Lenin and Philosophy and Other Essays*, London, Monthly Review Press, pp. 127–86.

AMERICAN ASSOCIATION OF COLLEGES FOR TEACHER EDUCATION (1973) 'No one model American', *Journal of Teacher Education*, 24, pp. 264–5.

ANTI-DEFAMATION LEAGUE OF B'NAI B'RITH (1986) *The Wonderful World of Difference: A Human Relations Program for Grades K-8*, New York, Anti-Defamation League of B'nai B'rith.

ANYON, J. (1979) 'Ideology and the United States history textbooks', *Harvard Educational Review*, 49, 3, pp. 361–86.

ANYON, J. (1983) 'Workers, labor and economic history, and textbook content', in APPLE, M.W. and WEIS, L. (Eds) *Ideology and Practice in Schooling*, Philadelphia, Temple University Press, pp. 37–60.

APPLE, M.W. (1979) *Ideology and Curriculum*, Boston, Routledge and Kegan Paul.

APPLE, M.W. (1982) *Education and Power*, Boston, Routledge and Kegan Paul.

APPLE, M.W. (1983) 'Curricular form and the logic of technical control', in APPLE, M.W. and WEIS, L. (Eds) *Ideology and Practice in Schooling*, Philadelphia, Temple University Press, pp. 143–65.

APPLE, M.W. (1986) *Teachers and Texts: A Political Economy of Class and Gender Relations in Education*, New York, Routledge and Kegan Paul.

APPLE, M.W. (1988) 'Redefining inequality: Authoritarian populism and the conservative restoration', *Teacher's College Record*, 90, 2, pp. 167–84.

APPLE, M.W. and BEYER, L. (Eds) (1988) *The Curriculum: Problems, Politics, and Possibilities*, Albany, State University of New York Press.

APPLE, M.W. and WEIS, L. (Eds) (1983) *Ideology and Practice in Schooling*, Philadelphia, Temple University Press.

APPLETON, N. (1983) *Cultural Pluralism in Education*, New York, Longman.

APTER, D. (1967) *The Politics of Modernization*, Chicago, University of Chicago Press.

ARNOT, M. (1981) *Class, Gender and Education*, Milton Keynes, Open University Press.

ARONOWITZ, S. and GIROUX, H. (1985) *Education Under Siege: The Conservative, Liberal, and Radical Debate Over Schooling*, South Hadley, Massachusetts, Bergin and Garvey.

ARROW, K.J. (1973) 'The theory of discrimination', in ASHENFELTER, O. and REES, A. (Eds) *Discrimination in Labor Markets*, Princeton, Princeton University Press.

ATKINSON, D., MORTEN, G. and SUE, D. (Eds) (1979) *Counseling American Minorities: A Cross-Cultural Perspective*, Dubuque, Iowa, William C. Brown.

AUSUBEL, D.P. (1964) 'How reversible are cognitive and motivational effects of cultural deprivation?' *Urban Education*, 1, pp. 16–39.

BAKER, G. (1973) 'Multicultural training for student teachers', *The Journal of Teacher Education*, 24, pp. 306–7.

BAKER, G. (1977) 'Development of the multicultural program: School of Education, University of Michigan', in KLASSEN, F.H. and GOLLNICK, D.M. (Eds) *Pluralism and the American Teacher: Issues and Case Studies*, Washington, D.C., Ethnic Heritage Center for Teacher Education of the American Association of Colleges for Teacher Education, pp. 163–9.

BALDWIN, J. (1986) *Nobody Knows My Name*, New York, Dell.

BANKS, J. (1973) *Teaching Ethnic Studies: Concepts and Strategies*, Washington, D.C., National Council for the Social Studies.

BANKS, J. (1981) *Multiethnic Education: Theory and Practice*, Boston, Allyn and Bacon.

BANKS, J. (1987) *Teaching Strategies for Ethnic Studies*, Boston, Allyn and Bacon.

BARAN, P. (1957) *The Political Economy of Growth*, New York, Monthly Review Press.

BARAN, P. and SWEEZY, M. (1966) *Monopoly Capital*, New York, Monthly Review Press.

BARRETT, M. (1980) *Women's Oppression: Problems in Marxist Feminist Analysis*, London, Verso.

BARTHES, R. (1975) *The Pleasure of the Text*, New York, Hill and Wang.

BASTIAN, A., FRUCHTER, N., GITTELL, M., GREER, C. and HASKINS, K. (1986) *Choosing Equality*, Philadelphia, Temple University Press.

BECKER, G.S. (1957) *The Economics of Discrimination*, Chicago, University of Chicago Press.

BEECHEY, V. (1985) 'Familial ideology', in BEECHEY, V. and DONALD, J. (Eds) *Subjectivity and Social Relations*, Milton Keynes, Open University Press, pp. 98–120.

BELL, R. (1975) 'Lower class negro mothers' aspirations for their children', in STUB, H. (Ed.) *The Sociology of Education: A Sourcebook*, Homewood, Illinois, Dorsey Press, pp. 125–36.

References

BELSEY, C. (1980) *Critical Practice*, London, Methuen.
BEN-TOVIM, G., GABRIEL, J., LAW, I. and STREDDER, K. (1981) 'Race, left strategies and the state', in ADLAM, D. *et al.* (Eds) *Politics and Power Three: Sexual Politics, Feminism, and Socialism*, London, Routledge and Kegan Paul, pp. 153–81.
BEN-TOVIM, G., GABRIEL, J., LAW, I. and STREDDER, K. (1982) 'A political analysis of race in the 1980s', in HUSBAND, C. (Ed.) *Race in Britain: Continuity and Change*, London, Hutchinson, pp. 303–16.
BERLOWITZ, M. (1984) 'Multicultural education; Fallacies and alternatives', in BERLOWITZ, M. and EDARI, R. (Eds) *Racism and the Denial of Human Rights: Beyond Ethnicity*, Minneapolis, Marxism Educational Press, pp. 37–52.
BERLOWITZ, M. and DURAND, H. (1980) 'Beyond court-ordered desegregation: School dropouts or student pushouts?' in BERLOWITZ, M. and CHAPMAN, F. (Eds) *The United States Educational System: Marxist Approaches*, Minneapolis, Marxism Educational Press, pp. 37–52.
BERNSTEIN, B. (1977) *Class, Codes and Control* (Volume 3), London, Routledge and Kegan Paul.
BERNSTEIN, B. (1982) 'Codes, modalities and the process of cultural reproduction: A model', in APPLE, M.W. (Ed.) *Cultural and Economic Reproduction in Education*, Boston, Routledge and Kegan Paul, pp. 304–55.
BLACKBURN, R. and MANN, M. (1979) *The Working Class in the Labor Market*, London, Macmillan.
BLAU, P. and DUNCAN, O. (1967) *The American Occupational Structure*, New York, Wiley.
BLAUNER, R. (1972) *Racial Oppression in America*, New York, Harper and Row.
BLOOM, A. (1987) *The Closing of the American Mind*, New York, Simon and Schuster.
BLOOM, B., DAVIS, A. and HESS, R. (1965) *Compensatory Education for Cultural Deprivation*, New York, Holt.
BOBBIT, F. (1924) *How to Make a Curriculum*, Boston, Houghton Mifflin.
BONACICH, E. (1980) 'Class approaches to ethnicity and race', *Insurgent Sociologist*, 10, pp. 9–24.
BONACICH, E. (1981) 'Capitalism and race relations in South Africa: A split labor market analysis', in ZEITLIN, M. (Ed.) *Political Power and Social Theory* (Volume 2), Greenwich, Connecticut, JAI Press, pp. 239–77.
BORDIEU, P. and PASSERON, J. (1977) *Reproduction in Education, Society and Culture*, London, Sage.
BOWLES, S. and GINTIS, H. (1976) *Schooling in Capitalist America*, New York, Basic Books.
BROOKS, C. (1966) 'Some approaches to teaching English as a second language', in WEBSTER, S. (Ed.) *The Disadvantaged Learner*, San Francisco, Chandler.
BROWN, K. (1985) 'Turning a blind eye: Racial oppression and the unintended consequences of white non-racism', *Sociological Review*, 33, pp. 670–90.
BUCKINGHAM, D. (1984) 'The whites of their eyes: A case study in responses

to educational television', in STRAKER-WELDS, M. (Ed.) *Education for a Multicultural Society*, London, Bell and Hyman, pp. 137–43.

BULLIVANT, B. (1981) *The Pluralist Dilemma in Education*, Sydney, Allen and Unwin.

BURAWOY, M. (1981) 'The capitalist state in South Africa: Marxist and sociological perspectives on race and class', in ZEITLIN, M. (Ed.) *Political Power and Social Theory* (Volume 2), Greenwich, Connecticut, JAI Press, pp. 279–335.

CARBY, H. (1982) 'Schooling in Babylon', in Centre for Contemporary Cultural Studies (Eds) *The Empire Strikes Back: Race and Racism in '70s Britain*, London, Hutchinson, pp. 183–211.

CAREW, J. (1984) 'Fulcrums of change', *Race and Class*, 26, 2, pp. 1–14.

CARMICHAEL, S. and HAMILTON, C. (1967) *Black Power*, New York, Vintage.

CARNOY, M. (Ed.) (1972) *Schooling in a Corporate Society*, New York, David McKay.

CARNOY, M. (1974) *Education and Cultural Imperialism*, New York, Longman.

CARNOY, M. (1982) 'Education, economy, and the state', in APPLE, M.W. (Ed.) *Cultural and Economic Reproduction in Education*, New York, Routledge and Kegan Paul, pp. 79–126.

CARNOY, M. (1984) *The State and Political Theory*, Princeton, Princeton University Press.

CARNOY, M. and LEVIN, H. (1985) *Schooling and Work in the Democratic State*, Stanford, Stanford University Press.

CASHMORE, E. and TROYNA, B. (1990) *Introduction to Race Relations*, Lewes, Falmer Press.

CHARTERS, W. (1926) 'Statement', in WHIPPLE, G. (Ed.) *The Foundations and Technique of Curriculum-Construction, Part II. The Foundations of Curriculum-Making. The Twenty-sixth Yearbook of the National Society for the Study of Education*, Bloomington, Illinois, Public School Publishing, p. 71.

CICOUREL, A. and KITSUSE, J. (1963) *The Educational Decision Makers*, Indianapolis, Bobbs-Merrill.

COLEMAN, J. (1966) *Equality of Educational Opportunity*, Washington, D.C., US Government.

CONNELL, R.W. (1987) Curriculum, politics, hegemony, and strategies of change. Unpublished Paper, Department of Sociology, Macquarie University.

CONNELL, R.W., et al. (1982) *Making the Difference: Schools, Families, and Social Division*, Boston, Allen and Unwin.

CORTES, C. (1973) 'Teaching the Chicano experience', in BANKS, J. (Ed.) *Teaching Ethnic Studies: Concepts and Strategies*, Washington, D.C., National Council for the Social Studies, pp. 181–99.

CORTES, C. (1986) 'The education of language minority students: A contextual interaction model', in California State Department of Education (Ed.) *Beyond Language: Social and Cultural Factors in Schooling Language Minority Students*, Los Angeles, Evaluation, Dissemination and Assessment Center, California State University, pp. 3–33.

References

COUNTS, G. (1932) *Dare the School Build a New Social Order?* New York, John Day.

CRICHLOW, W. (1985) Urban crisis, schooling, and black youth unemployment: A case study. Unpublished Paper, School of Education and Human Development, University of Rochester.

CRICHLOW, W. (1990) A social analysis of black youth commitment and disaffection in an urban high school. Unpublished Ed.D. Dissertation, School of Education and Human Development, University of Rochester.

CUBBERLEY, E.P. (1909) *Changing Conceptions of Education*, Boston, Houghton Mifflin.

DAHL, R. (1961) *Who Governs?* New Haven, Yale University Press.

DALE, R. (1982) 'Education and the capitalist state: Contributions and contradictions', in APPLE, M.W. (Ed.) *Cultural and Economic Reproduction in Education*, Boston, Routledge and Kegan Paul, pp. 127–61.

DAVIS, K. and MOORE, W. (1945) 'Some principles of stratification', *American Sociological Review*, 10, pp. 242–9.

DEUTSCH, M. and ASSOCIATES (1967) *The Disadvantaged Child: Selected Papers of Martin Deutsch and Associates*, New York, Basic Books.

DUNCAN, O., FEATHERSTONE, D. and DUNCAN, B. (1972) *Socioeconomic Background and Achievement*, New York, Academic Press.

DUNN, L. (1987) *Bilingual Hispanic Children on the US Mainland: A Review of Research on their Cognitive, Linguistic, and Scholastic Development*, Circle Pines, Minnesota, American Guidance Service.

DURKHEIM, E. (1977) *The Evolution of Educational Thought: Lectures on the Formation and Development of Secondary Education in France*, London, Routledge and Kegan Paul.

EAGLETON, T. (1983) *Literary Theory*, Minneapolis, University of Minnesota Press.

EASTON, D. (1965) *A Framework for Political Analysis*, Englewood Cliffs, New Jersey, Prentice-Hall.

ECO, U. (1976) *A Theory of Semiotics*, Bloomington, Indiana University Press.

EDARI, R. (1984) 'Racial minorities and forms of ideological mystification', in BERLOWITZ, M. and EDARI, R. (Eds) *Racism and the Denial of Human Rights: Beyond Ethnicity*, Minneapolis, Marxist Educational Press, pp. 7–18.

EDGERTON, S. (1989) Love in the margins: An 'epistemology of marginality' in Ellison's *Invisible Man* and Morrison's *Beloved*. Unpublished manuscript, Department of Curriculum and Instruction, Louisiana State University.

EDUCATION WEEK (1986) 'Here they come ready or not: An *Education Week* special report on the ways in which America's population in motion is changing the outlook for schools and society', *Education Week*, 14 May, pp. 14–28.

ELLISON, R. (1982) *Invisible Man*, New York, Random House.

ELSHTAIN, J. (1986) 'The new feminist scholarship', *Salmagundi*, 70–71, pp. 3–26.

EVERHART, R. (1983) *Reading, Writing and Resistance*, London, Routledge and Kegan Paul.

EYSENCK, J. and KAMIN, L. (1981) *The Intelligence Controversy*, New York, John Wiley and Sons.

FISH, J. (1981) The psychological impact of field work experiences and cognitive dissonance upon attitude change in a human relations program. Unpublished Ph.D. Dissertation, University of Wisconsin-Madison.

FISKE, J. (1987) *Television Culture*, London, Methuen.

FISKE, J. and HARTLEY, J. (1978) *Reading Television*, London, Methuen.

FITZGERALD, M. (1984) *Political Parties and Black People*, London, Runnymede Trust.

FOUCAULT, M. (1970) *The Order of Things: An Archeology of Human Sciences*, New York, Pantheon.

FOUCAULT, M. (1972) *The Archaeology of Knowledge*, New York, Harper Colophon.

FOUCAULT, M. (1977) *Discipline and Punish*, London, Allen Lane.

FORDHAM, S. (1990) 'Racelessness as a factor in Black students' school success: Pragmatic strategy or phyrrhic victory?' *Harvard Educational Review*, Reprint Series No. 21, pp. 232–62.

FREIRE, P. (1970) *Pedagogy of the Oppressed*, New York, Seabury Press.

FREIRE, P. (1985) *The Politics of Education*, Boston, Bergin and Garvey.

FRIEDMAN, M. (1962) *Capitalism and Freedom*, Chicago, University of Chicago Press.

FULLER, M. (1980) 'Black girls in a London comprehensive school', in DEEM, R. (Ed.) *Schooling for Women's Work*, London, Routledge and Kegan Paul, pp. 52–65.

GAMORAN, A. and BERENDS, M. (1986) *The Effects of Stratification in Secondary Schools: Synthesis of Survey and Ethnographic Research*, Madison, National Center on Effective Secondary Schools, University of Wisconsin-Madison.

GARCIA, E. (1974) 'Chicano cultural diversity: Implications for competency-based teacher education', in HUNTER, W. (Ed.) *Multicultural Education Through Competency-based Teacher Education*, Washington, D.C., American Association of Colleges for Teacher Education.

GARDNER, R. (1984) 'Human intelligence isn't what we think it is', *US News and World Report*, 19 March, pp. 77–8.

GIBSON, M. (1984) 'Approaches to multicultural education in the United States: Some concepts and assumptions', *Anthropology and Education Quarterly*, 15, pp. 94–119.

GILROY, P. (1982) 'Steppin' out of Babylon: Race, class, and autonomy', in Centre for Contemporary Cultural Studies (Eds) *The Empire Strikes Back*, London, Hutchinson, pp. 278–314.

GINTIS, H. (1980) 'Communication and politics: Marxism and the "problem" of liberal democracy', *Socialist Review*, 10, pp. 189–232.

GIROUX, H. (1981) *Ideology, Culture and the Process of Schooling*, Lewes, Falmer Press.

GIROUX, H. (1983) *Theory and Resistance in Education: A Pedagogy for the Opposition*, South Hadley, Massachusetts, Bergin and Garvey.

GIROUX, H. (1985) 'Introduction', in FREIRE, P. *The Politics of Education*, South Hadley, Massachusetts, Bergin and Garvey.

GLAZER, N. and MOYNIHAN, D. (1963) *Beyond the Melting Pot*, Cambridge, Harvard University Press.

GLAZER, N. and MOYNIHAN, D. (Eds) (1975) *Ethnicity: Theory and Experience*, Cambridge, Massachusetts, Harvard University Press.

GLISSANT, E. (1981) *Monsieur Toussaint: A Play*, (trans. J. Silenicks) Washington, D.C., Three Continents Press.

GOBINEAU, J. (1915) *The Inequality of Human Races*, London, Heineman.

GODDARD, H. (1912) *The Kallikak Family: A Study in the Heredity of Feeble-mindedness*, New York, Macmillan.

GOLLNICK, D.M. (1980) 'Multicultural education', *Viewpoints in Teaching and Learning*, 56, pp. 1–17.

GOODLAD, J. (1983) *A Place Called School: Prospects for the Future*, New York, McGraw-Hill.

GOTTFRIED, N. (1973) 'Effects of early intervention programs', in MILLER, K. and DREGER, R. (Eds) *Comparative Studies of Blacks and Whites*, New York, Seminar Press, pp. 273–93.

GOULD, S. (1981) *The Mismeasure of Man*, New York, W.W. Norton.

GRAMSCI, A. (1983) *Selection from the Prison Notebooks*, New York, International Publishers.

GRANT, C. (1975) 'Exploring the contours of a multicultural education', in GRANT, C. (Ed.) *Sifting and Winnowing: An Exploration of the Relationship between CBTE and Multicultural Education*, Madison, Teacher Corps Associates, University of Wisconsin-Madison, pp. 1–11.

GRANT, C. (1978) 'Education that is multicultural — Isn't that what we mean?' *Journal of Teacher Education*, 29, pp. 45–8.

GRANT, C. and SLEETER, C. (1985) 'The literature on multicultural education: Review and analysis', *Educational Review*, 37, 2, pp. 97–118.

GRANT, C. and SLEETER, C. (1986) 'Race, class, and gender in education', *Review of Educational Research*, 56, pp. 195–211.

GRANT, C. and SLEETER, C. (1989) *Turning on Learning: Five Approaches for Multicultural Teaching Plans for Race, Class, Gender, and Disability*, Columbus, Merrill.

GRANT, L. (1984) 'Black females' "place" in desegregated classrooms', *Sociology of Education*, 57, pp. 98–111.

GRANT, L. (1985) Uneasy alliances: Black males, teachers, and peers in desegregated classroom. Unpublished Manuscript, Department of Sociology, Southern Illinois University.

GREENBERG, S. (1980) *Race and State in Capitalist Development: Comparative Perspectives*, New Haven, Yale University Press.

GREENE, M. (1971) 'Curriculum and consciousness', *Teachers College Record*, 73, pp. 253–69.

HALL, S. (1980) 'Race, articulation, and societies structured in dominance', in UNESCO (Eds) *Sociological Theories: Race and Colonialism*, Paris, UNESCO, pp. 305–45.

HALL, S. (1981) 'Teaching Race', in JAMES, A. and JEFFCOATE, R. (Eds) *The School in the Multicultural Society*, London, Harper and Row, pp. 58–69.

HALL, S. (1986) 'Gramsci's relevance to the analysis of race', *Communication Inquiry*, 10, pp. 5–27.

HALL, S. (1988) 'The toad in the garden: Thatcherism among the theorists', in NELSON, C. and GROSSBERG, L. (Eds) *Marxism and the Interpretation of Culture*, Illinois, University of Illinois Press, pp. 35–74.

HALL, S.G. (1904) *Adolescence: Its Psychology and its Relations to Physiology, Anthropology, Sociology, Sex, Crime, Religion and Education*, New York, Appleton.

HANN, A., DANZBERGER, J. and LEFKOWITZ, B. (1987) *Dropouts in America*, Washington, D.C., Institute for Educational Leadership.

HARRIS, M. (1968) *The Rise of Anthropological Theory*, New York, Thomas Crowell.

HEATH, S.B. (1986) 'Sociocultural contexts of language development', in California State Department of Education (Ed.) *Beyond Language: Social and Cultural Factors in Schooling Language Minority Students*, Los Angeles, Evaluation, Dissemination and Assessment Center, California State University, pp. 143–86.

HECHTER, M. (1975) *Internal Colonialism: The Celtic Fringe in British National Development 1536–1966*, Berkeley, University of California Press.

HENRIQUES, J. (1984) 'Social psychology and the politics of racism', in HENRIQUES, J. (Ed.) *Changing the Subject*, London, Methuen, pp. 60–89.

HESS, R. and SHIPMAN, V. (1975) 'Early experience and socialization of cognitive modes in children', in STUB, H. (Ed.) *The Sociology of Education: A Sourcebook*, Homewood, Illinois, Dorsey Press, pp. 96–113.

HICKS, E. (1981) 'Cultural Marxism: Nonsynchrony and feminist practice', in SARGENT, L. (Ed.) *Women and Revolution*, Boston, South End Press, pp. 219–38.

HIRSCH, E.D. (1987) *Cultural Literacy: What Every American Needs to Know*, Boston, Houghton Mifflin.

HOGAN, D. (1982) 'Education and class formation: The peculiarities of the Americans', in APPLE, M.W. (Ed.) *Cultural and Economic Reproduction in Education*, Boston, Routledge and Kegan Paul, pp. 32–78.

HOLLWAY, W. (1989) *Subjectivity and Method in Psychology: Gender, Meaning and Science*, London, Sage.

HUEBNER, D. (1968) 'Implications of psychological thought for curriculum', in UNRUH, G., and LEEPER, R. (Eds) *Influences in Curriculum Change*, Washington, D.C., Association for Supervision, pp. 28–37.

HUNT, J. (1964) 'The psychological basis for using pre-school enrichment as an antidote for cultural deprivation', *The Merrill-Palmer Quarterly*, 10, pp. 209–48.

HUNTER, A. (1986) Children in the service of conservatism, Unpublished Paper, Department of History, University of Wisconsin-Madison.

HURN, C. (1979) *The Limits and Possibilities of Schooling: An Introduction to the Sociology of Education*, Boston, Allyn and Bacon.

HURSTON, Z.N. (1978) *Their Eyes Were Watching God*, Urbana, University of Illinois Press.

ILLICH, I. (1970) *De-schooling Society*, New York, Harper and Row.

IRIGARAY, L. (1985) *This Sex Which Is Not One*, Ithaca, New York, Cornell University Press.

JACKUBOWICZ, A. (1985) 'State and ethnicity: multiculturalism as ideology', in RIZVI, F. (Ed) *Multiculturalism as an Educational Policy*, Geelong, Victoria, Deakin University Press, pp. 43–63.

JACOB, J. (1988) 'Black America 1987: An overview', in National Urban League (Eds) *The State of Black America 1988*, New York, National Urban League, pp. 1–6.

JAMES, C.L.R. (1980) *Spheres of Existence: Selected Writings*, Westport, Connecticut, Hill Company.

JANMOHAMED, A. (1987) 'Introduction: Toward a theory of minority discourse', *Cultural Critique*, 6, pp. 5–11.

JANMOHAMED, A. and LLOYD, D. (1987) 'Introduction: Minority discourse — what is to be done', *Cultural Critique*, 7, pp. 5–17.

JENCKS, C. (1972) *Inequality: A Reassessment of the Effect of the Family and Schooling in America*, New York, Harper and Row.

JENSEN, A. (1969) 'How much can we boost IQ and scholastic achievement?' *Harvard Educational Review*, Reprint Series No. 2, pp. 1–23.

JENSEN, A. (1981) *Straight Talk About Mental Tests*, New York, Free Press.

JENSEN, A. (1984) 'Political ideologies and educational research', *Phi Delta Kappan*, 65, 7, p. 460.

JORDAN, J. (1980) *Passion*, Boston, Beacon Press.

JORDAN, W. (1968) *White over Black: American Attitudes Toward the Negro, 1550–1812*, Baltimore, Penguin Books.

KAESTLE, C. (1973) *The Evolution of an Urban School System, New York City, 1750–1850*, Cambridge, Harvard University Press.

KAESTLE, C. (1983) *Pillars of the Republic: Common Schools and American Society, 1780–1860*, New York, Hill and Wang.

KAGAN, S. (1986) 'Cooperative learning and sociocultural factors in schooling', in California State Department of Education (Ed.) *Beyond Language: Social and Cultural Factors in Schooling Language Minority Students*, Los Angeles, Evaluation, Dissemination and Assessment Center, California State University, pp. 231–98.

KARABEL, J. and HALSEY, A. (Eds) (1977) *Power and Ideology in Education*, New York, Oxford University Press.

KING, E. (1980) *Teaching Ethnic Awareness*, Santa Monica, Good Year.

KLEINFIELD, J. (1975) 'Positive stereotyping: The cultural relativist in the classroom', *Human Organization*, 34, pp. 269–74.

KLIEBARD, H. (1986) *The Struggle for the American Curriculum 1893–1958*, Boston, Routledge and Kegan Paul.

KUHN, A. (1982) *Women's Pictures: Feminism and Cinema*, London, Routledge and Kegan Paul.

KUHN, T. (1970) *The Structure of Scientific Revolutions*, Chicago, University of Chicago Press.

LACLAU, E. and MOUFFE, C. (1982) 'Recasting Marxism: Hegemony and new political movements', *Socialist Review*, 66, 12, pp. 91–113.

LACLAU, E. and MOUFFE, C. (1985) *Hegemony and Socialist Strategy: Toward a Radical Democratic Politics*, London, Verso.

LEWIS C. (1976) 'The multi-cultural education model and minorities: Some reservations', *Anthropological Quarterly*, 7, pp. 32–7.

LOEHLIN, J., LINDZEY, G. and SPUHLER, J. (1975) *Race Differences in Intelligence*, San Francisco, W.H. Freeman.

LORD, M. (1987) 'Frats and sororities: The Greek rites of exclusion', *The Nation*, 245, 1, pp. 10–13.

LOURY, G. (1985) 'The moral quandary of the black community', *In The Public Interests*, 75, p. 19.

MACDONALD, J. and LEEPER, R. (1966) *Language and Meaning*, Washington, D.C., Association for Supervision and Curriculum Development.

MANN, H. (1957) *The Republic and the School: Horace Mann on the Education of Freemen*, Ed. L. CREMIN, New York, Bureau of Publications, Teachers College, Columbia University.

MARABLE, M. (1983) *How Capitalism Underdeveloped Black America: Problems in Race, Political Economy and Society*, Boston, South End Press.

MARABLE, M. (1985) *Black American Politics*, London, Verso.

MCCARTHY, C. (1988) 'Reconsidering liberal and radical perspectives on racial inequality in schooling: Making the case for nonsynchrony', *Harvard Educational Review* 58, 2, pp. 265–79.

MCCARTHY, C. and APPLE, M.W. (1988) 'Race, class, and gender in American educational research: Toward a nonsynchronous parallelist position', in WEIS, L. (Ed.) *Class, Race and Gender in American Education*, Albany, State University of New York, pp. 9–39.

MCLAREN, P. and DANTLEY, M. (in press) 'Leadership and a critical pedagogy of race: Cornel West, Stuart Hall, and the prophetic tradition', *Journal of Negro Education*.

MCNEIL, L. (1983) 'Defensive teaching and classroom control', in APPLE, M.W. and WEIS, L. (Eds) *Ideology and Practice in Schooling*, Philadelphia, Temple University Press pp. 114–42.

MCROBBIE, A. (1978) 'Working class girls and the culture of femininity', in Center for Contemporary Cultural Studies, (Eds) *Women Take Issue*, London, Hutchinson, pp. 96–108.

MONTALTO, N. (1981) 'Multicultural education in the New York City public schools, 1919–41', in RAVITCH, D. and GOODENOW, R. (Eds) *Educating an Urban People: The New York City Experience*, New York, Teachers College Press, pp. 67–83.

MORTON, S. (1839) *Crania Americana or, a Comparative View of the Skulls of Various Aboriginal Nations of North and South America*, Philadelphia, John Pennington.

MOYNIHAN, D. (1965) *The Negro Family: The Case for National Action*, Washington, D.C., United States Department of Labor, Office of Policy, Planning, and Research.

MULLARD, C. (1985) 'Racism in society and school; History, policy, and practice', in RIZVI, F. (Ed.) *Multiculturalism as Educational Policy*, Geelong, Victoria, Deakin University Press, pp. 64–81.

MURPHY, L. and LIVINGSTONE, J. (1985) 'Racism and the limits of radical feminism', *Race and Class*, 26, 4, pp. 61–70.

MURRAY, C. (1984) *Losing Ground*, New York, Basic Books.

MYRDAL, G. (1944) *An American Dilemma*, New York, Harper and Row.

NATIONAL COMMISSION ON EXCELLENCE IN EDUCATION (1983) *A Nation at Risk: The Imperative for Educational Reform*, Washington, D.C., US Department of Education.

NEWSWEEK (1988) 'Caveman Smarts', *Newsweek*, 30 May, p. 59.

NIETZSCHE, F. (1967) *On the Genealogy of Morals*, (trans. W. KAUFMAN and R. HOLINDALE), New York, Vintage Books.

References

NKOMO, M. (1984) *Student Culture and Activism in Black South African Universities*, Wesport, Connecticut, Greenwood Press.

O'BRIEN, M. (1984) 'The commatization of women: Patriarchal fetishism in the sociology of education', *Interchange*, 15, 2, pp. 43–60.

O'CONNOR, D. and SODERLIND, E. (1983) *The Swedes: In their Homeland, in America, in Connecticut. The Peoples of Connecticut Multicultural Ethnic Heritage Series, Number Seven*, Storrs, Connecticut, Thut (I.N.) World Education Center, University of Connecticut.

OFFE, C. (1984) *Contradictions of the Welfare State*, London, Hutchinson.

OGBU, J. (1978) *Minority Education and Caste*, New York, Academic Press.

OGBU, J. and MATUTE-BIANCHI, M. (1986) 'Understanding sociocultural factors in education: Knowledge, identity, and school adjustment', in CALIFORNIA STATE DEPARTMENT OF EDUCATION (Ed.) *Beyond Language: Social and Cultural Factors in Schooling Language Minority Students*, Los Angeles, Evaluation, Dissemination and Assessment Center, California State University, pp. 73–142.

OLNECK, M. (1983) Ethnicity, pluralism, and American schooling, Unpublished Paper, Department of Educational Policy Studies, University of Wisconsin-Madison, Madison, Wisconsin.

OLNECK, M. (1989) The recurring dream: Symbolism and ideology in intercultural and multicultural education. Paper presented at the meeting of the American Educational Research Association, San Francisco.

OLNECK, M. and LAZERSON, M. (1980) 'Education', in THERNSTROM, S. *et al.* (Eds) *Harvard Encyclopedia of American Ethnic Groups*, Cambridge, Harvard University Press, pp. 303–19.

OMI, M. and WINANT, H. (1981) 'New wave dread: Immigration and intra-Third World conflict', *Socialist Review*, 60, pp. 77–87.

OMI, M. and WINANT, H. (1983) 'By the rivers of Babylon: Race in the United State — Part one', *Socialist Review*, 72, pp. 31–63.

OMI, M. and WINANT, H. (1986) *Racial Formation in the United States*, New York, Routledge and Kegan Paul.

ORR, E.W. (1987) *Twice as Less*, New York, W.W. Norton.

OXFORD UNIVERSITY PRESS (1980) *Oxford American Dictionary*, New York, Oxford University Press.

PARMAR, P. (1982) 'Gender, race, class: Asian women in resistance', in Centre for Contemporary Cultural Studies (Eds) *The Empire Strikes Back: Race and Racism in '70s Britain*, London, Hutchinson, pp. 236–75.

PATTERSON, O. (1977) *Ethnic Chauvinism: The Reactionary Impulse*, New York, Stein and Day.

PETTIGREW, L.E. (1974) 'Competency-based teacher education: Teacher training for multicultural education', in HUNTER, W. (Ed.) *Multicultural Education through Competency-based Teacher Education*, Washington, D.C., American Association of Colleges of Teacher Education.

PETTIGREW, T. (1969) 'The negro and education: Problems and proposals', in KATZ, I. and GURIN, P. (Eds) *Race and the Social Sciences*, New York, Basic Books, pp. 49–112.

PIVEN, F. and CLOWARD, R. (1979) *Poor People's Movements: How They Succeed, Why They Fail*, New York, Vintage.

POPKEWITZ, T. (1984) *Paradigm and Ideology in Educational Research*, Lewes, Falmer Press.

POPKEWITZ, T. (1987) *The Formation of School Subjects*, Lewes, Falmer Press.

POSTER, M. (1984) *Foucault, Marxism and History*, Oxford, Polity Press.

POULANTZAS, N. (1975) *Classes in Contemporary Capitalism*, London, New Left Books.

RAMIREZ, M. and CASTANEDA, A. (1974) *Cultural Democracy, Bicognitive Development, and Education*, New York, Academic Press.

RASKIN, M. (1971) *Being and Doing*, New York, Random House.

REICH, M. (1981) *Racial Inequality*, Princeton, Princeton University Press.

REX, J. (1983) *Race Relations in Sociological Theory*, London, Routledge and Kegan Paul.

RIESMAN, D., GLAZER, N. and DENNEY, R. (1969) *The Lonely Crowd*, New Haven, Yale University Press.

RIST, R. (1970) 'Social class and teacher expectations: The self-fulfilling prophecy in ghetto education', *Harvard Educational Review*, 40, pp. 441–51.

RIZVI, F. (Ed.) (1985) *Multiculturalism as an Educational Policy*, Geelong, Victoria, Deakin University Press.

ROEMER, J. (1979) 'Divide and conquer: Microfoundations of Marxian theory of wage discrimination', *Bell Journal of Economics*, 10, pp. 695–705.

ROMAN, L., CHRISTIAN-SMITH, L. and ELLSWORTH, E. (1988) *Becoming Feminine: The Politics of Popular Culture*, Lewes, Falmer Press.

ROSENTHAL, R. and JACOBSON, L. (1968) *Pygmalion in the Classroom*, New York, Holt, Rinehart, and Winston.

ROSS, E.A. (1901) *Social Control: A Survey of the Foundations of Order*, New York, Macmillan.

RUGG, H.O. (1932) 'Social reconstruction through education', *Progressive Education*, 9, pp. 11–18.

RUSHER, W. (1975) *The Making of a New Majority*, Ottawa, Illinois, Greenhill Publications.

RUSHTON, J. (1981) 'Careers and the multicultural curriculum', in LYNCH, J. (Ed.) *Teaching in the Multicultural School*, London, Ward Lock, pp. 163–70.

SAID, E. (1986) 'Intellectuals in the post-colonial world', *Salmagundi*, 70–71, pp. 44–64.

SAID, E. (1989) 'Representing the colonized: Anthropology's interlocutors', *Critical Inquiry*, 15, 2, pp. 205–25.

SARUP, M. (1986) *The Politics of Multi-racial Education*, London, Routledge and Kegan Paul.

SAUL, J. (1979) *The State and Revolution in Eastern Africa*, New York, Monthly Review Press.

SCHMIDT, P. (1989) 'Educators foresee "renaissance" in African studies', *Education Week*, 18 October, p. 8.

SCOTT, J.C. and KERKVLIET, T. (Eds) (1986) *Everyday Forms of Peasant Resistance in South East Asia*, London, Frank Case.

SELDEN, S. (1985) 'Educational policy and biological science', *Teachers College Record*, 87, pp. 35–51.

SELDEN, S. (1988) 'Biological determinism and the normal school curriculum: Helen Putnam and the NEA committee on racial well-being, 1910–22', in PINAR, W. (Ed.) *Contemporary Curriculum Discourses*, Scottsdale, Arizona, Gorsuch Scarisbrick Publishers, pp. 50–65.

SEWELL, W. and HAUSER, R. (1975) *Education, Occupation and Earnings*, New York, Academic Press.

SEXTON, P. (1961) *Education and Income*, New York, Viking.

SHANGE, N. (1983) *A Daughter's Geography*, New York, St. Martin's Press.

SHOR, I. (1980) *Critical Teaching and Everyday Life*, Boston, South End Press.

SIMPSON, L. (1987) 'Values, respect, and recognition: On race and culture in the neoconservative debate', *Praxis International*, 7, pp. 164–73.

SIZER, T. (1984) *Horace's Compromise: The Dilemma of the American High School*, Boston, Houghton Mifflin.

SLEETER, C. and GRANT, C. (1986) The literature on multicultural education in the USA. Paper presented at the meeting of the American Educational Research Association, San Francisco.

SMALL-MCCARTHY, R. (1988) 'Racism in the schools: Breaking the silence', *Rethinking Schools*, 2, 4, p. 18.

SMITH, V. (1988) 'Busing: How to get everyone mad', *Newsweek*, 7 March, pp. 39–40.

SNEDDEN, D. (1921) *Sociological Determination of Objectives in Education*, Philadelphia, J.B. Lippincott.

SOWELL, T. (1975) *Race and Economics*, New York, David McKay.

SOWELL, T. (1977) 'New light on the black IQ controversy', *New York Times Magazine*, 27 March, pp. 56–63.

SOWELL, T. (1981) *Ethnic America*, New York, Basic Books.

SPENCER, D. (1984) 'The home and school lives of women teachers', *The Elementary School Journal*, 84, pp. 293–8.

SPENCER, H. (1892) *Essays: Scientific, Political and Speculative*, New York, D. Appleton.

SPRING, J.H. (1972) *Education and the Rise of the Corporate State*, Boston, Beacon Press.

SPRING, J.H. (1985) *American Education: An Introduction to Social and Political Aspects*, New York, Longman.

STEELE, S. (1989) 'The recoloring of campus life: Student racism, academic pluralism, and the end of a dream', *Harper's Magazine* (February), pp. 47–55.

STODOLSKY, S. and LESSER, G. (1967) 'Learning patterns in the disadvantaged', *Harvard Educational Review*, 37, pp. 546–93.

SUDARKASA, N. (1988) 'Black enrollment in higher education: The unfulfilled promise of equality', in NATIONAL URBAN LEAGUE (Eds) *The State of Black America 1988*, New York, National Urban League, pp. 7–22.

SUE, S. and PADILLA, A. (1986) 'Ethnic minority issues in the United States: Challenges for the educational system', in CALIFORNIA STATE DEPARTMENT OF EDUCATION (Ed.) *Beyond Language: Social and Cultural Factors in Schooling Language Minority Students*, Los Angeles, Evaluation, Dissemination and Assessment Center, California State University pp. 35–72.

SUZUKI, B.H. (1979) 'Multicultural education: What's it all about?' *Integrated Education*, 97, pp. 43–50.

SUZUKI, B.H. (1984) 'Curriculum transformation for multicultural education', *Education and Urban Society*, 16, pp. 294–322.

SWARTZ, E. (1989) *Multicultural Curriculum Development*, Rochester, New York, Rochester City School District.

SWINTON, D. (1988) 'Economic status of blacks 1987', in NATIONAL URBAN LEAGUE (Eds) *The State of Black America 1988*, New York, National Urban League, pp. 129–52.

TAXEL, J. (1983) 'The American revolution in children's fiction: Analysis of literary content, form, and ideology', in APPLE M. and WEIS, L. (Eds) *Ideology and Practice in Schooling*, Philadelphia, Temple University Press, pp. 61–8.

TERMAN, L. (1916) *The Measurement of Intelligence*, Boston, Houghton Mifflin.

THOMAS, W.I. (1928) *The Child in America*, New York, Knopf.

THOMPSON, E.P. (1966) *The Making of the Working Class*, New York, Vintage Books.

TIEDT, I. and TIEDT, P. (1986) *Multicultural Teaching: A Handbook of Activities, Information, and Resources*, Boston, Allyn Bacon.

TIFFT, S. (1989) 'Bigots in the ivory tower', *Time Magazine*, 23 January, p. 48.

TROYNA, B. (1984) 'Multicultural education: Emancipation or containment?' in BARTON, L. and WALKER, S. (Eds) *Social Crisis and Educational Research*, London, Croom Helm, pp. 75–97.

TROYNA, B. and WILLIAMS, J. (1986) *Racism, Education, and the State*, London, Croom Helm.

UNIVERSITY OF WISCONSIN-MADISON STEERING COMMITTEE ON MINORITY AFFAIRS (1987) *Final Report*, Madison, University of Wisconsin-Madison.

VALLI, L. (1983) 'Becoming clerical workers: Business education and the culture of femininity', in APPLE, M.W. and WEIS, L. (Eds) *Ideology and Practice in Schooling*, Philadelphia, Temple University Press, pp. 213–34.

VIADERO, D. (1989) 'Schools witness a troubling revival of bigotry', *Education Week*, 24 May, p. 1.

VENN, C. (1984) 'The subject of psychology', in HENRIQUES, J. (Ed.) *Changing the Subject*, London, Methuen, pp. 119–52.

WALKERDINE, V. (1984) 'Developmental psychology and the child-centered pedagogy: The insertion of Piaget into early education', in HENRIQUES, J. (Ed.) *Changing the Subject*, London, Methuen, pp. 135–202.

WEIS, L. (1983) 'Schooling and cultural production: A comparison of black and white lived culture', in APPLE, M. and WEIS, L. (Eds) *Ideology and Practice in Schooling*, Philadelphia, Temple University Press, pp. 235–61.

WEIS, L. (Ed.) (1988) *Class, Race, and Gender in American Education*, Albany, State University of New York Press.

WELLMAN, D. (1977) *Portraits of White Racism*, Cambridge, Cambridge University Press.

WEST, C. (1982) *Prophesy and Deliverance: Toward a Revolutionary Afro-American Christianity*, Philadelphia, Westminister Press.

WEST, C. (1988) 'Marxist theory and the specificity of Afro-American oppression', in NELSON, C. and GROSSBERG, L. (Eds) *Marxism and the*

Interpretation of Culture, Urbana, Illinois, University of Illinois Press, pp. 17–33.

WEXLER, P. (1976) *The Sociology of Education: Beyond Equality*, Indianapolis, Bobbs-Merrill.

WEXLER, P. (1982) 'Structure, text and subject: A critical sociology of school knowledge', in APPLE, M.W. (Ed.) *Cultural and Economic Reproduction in Education*, Boston, Routledge and Kegan Paul, pp. 275–303.

WEXLER, P. (1987) *Social Analysis and Education: After the New Sociology*, New York, Routledge and Kegan Paul.

WHITTY, G. (1985) *Sociology and School Knowledge*, London, Methuen.

WIGGAM, A.E. (1924) *The Fruit of the Family Tree*, Indianapolis, Bobbs-Merrill.

WILLIAMS, E. (1964) *Capitalism and Slavery*, London, Andre Deutsch.

WILLIAMS, M. (1982) 'Multicultural/pluralistic education: Public education in America "The way it's 'spoze to be'"', *Clearing House*, 3, pp. 131–5.

WILLIAMS, R. (1961) *The Long Revolution*, London, Verso.

WILLIAMS, R. (1976) *Key Words: A Vocabulary of Culture and Society*, New York, Oxford University Press.

WILLIS, P. (1981) *Learning to Labor*, New York, Columbia University Press.

WISCONSIN DEPARTMENT OF PUBLIC INSTRUCTION (1986) *A Guide to Curriculum Planning in Social Studies*, Madison, Wisconsin, Wisconsin Department of Public Instruction.

WOOD, G. (1985) 'Schooling in a democracy: Transformation or reproduction', in RIZVI, F. (Ed.) *Multiculturalism as an Educational Policy*, Geelong, Victoria, Deakin University, pp. 91–111.

WRIGHT, E.O. (1978) *Class, Crisis, and the State*, London, New Left Review.

YOUNG, M.F.D. (Ed.) (1971) *Knowledge and Control: New Directions for the Sociology of Education*, London, Collier-Macmillan.

Index